Disclaimer

Table of contents

Introduction

Tired of the endless cycle of bland, uninspiring meals that come with most health-conscious diets? Fed up with spending money on cookbooks promising thousands of days' worth of recipes, only to find less than a hundred, most of which barely differ by an ingredient or two? Have you had enough of cookbooks without any delicious photos of the dishes? If so, this book is exactly what you need.

My name is Sandra Trivett, and I am a professional cook specializing in crafting menus for various diets. I'm also a mother of four and fully understand the challenge of preparing healthy and quick meals. Dishes that are both delicious and nutritious appeal to my children and my husband, who follows a low-sodium diet. That's why I created this book, selecting the best of my low-sodium air fryer recipes to share with you. But first, let me tell you a bit more about who this book is for.

Why Low Sodium?

A low-sodium diet is often recommended for a variety of health conditions. It's not just a fad; it's a neces-sity for many. High sodium intakes linked with increased risks of hypertension, heart disease, and kidney problems. If you find yourself in this category or are simply health-conscious, this cookbook is your perfect companion.

The Magic of Air Fryer Cooking

The air fryer is more than just a trendy kitchen gadget; it's a pivotal tool in revolutionizing how we approach healthy cooking, especially for low-sodium diets. But why does it fit the best? Firstly, the air fryer's rapid air technology cooks food by circulating hot air around it. This creates a crispy layer that mimics the satisfying texture of fried foods. Therefore, you can enjoy your favorite dishes without the added sodium often found in traditional frying methods. Secondly, this cooking method enhances the ingredients' natural flavors, reducing the need to rely on salt for taste. As a result, each dish retains its authentic taste while adhering to your dietary needs. Lastly, the air fryer is incredibly versatile, making it ideal for various recipes – from crispy vegetables to tender meats, all cooked to perfection with minimal sodium. This versatility ensures that following a low-sodium diet doesn't mean compromising on variety or pleasure in eating.

From My Kitchen

In theory, cooking low-sodium meals with an air fryer sounds fantastic, but in practice, the results aren't always as remarkable as the gadget's advertisements might suggest. And it's true, finding the perfect balance requires experimentation and testing various recipes until you hit that sweets pot of taste and health – much like any culinary endeavor. But guess what? I have great news for you – I've done all that hard work on your behalf.

This book is a culmination of my journey, experimenting and perfecting each recipe to ensure you get the best possible outcome from your air fryer without trial and error. You won't find hundreds of repetitive recipes here. Instead, I offer a collection of about 100 carefully crafted, diverse recipes. From succulent fish dishes and hearty meats to delightful desserts, each recipes distinct and tailored to fit a low-sodium diet without compromising on flavor.

Moreover, each recipe comes with a vibrant photograph, so you know exactly what you're aiming for. I've also taken the extra step to label each dish clearly – whether it's spicy, gluten-free, vegan, or vegetarian. This way, you can easily find recipes that suit your dietary needs and preferences.

Share Your Experience

Understanding Recipe Icons

In navigating the diverse array of recipes within this cookbook, it's helpful to pay attention to the accompanying icons. Each recipe is adorned with symbols denoting its attributes:

Every recipe includes clear "Notes" where these icons are prominently displayed, ensuring you can easily identify the nature of each dish before diving into the cooking process. These visual cues areconveniently listed in the table of contents, enabling you to swiftly identify recipes tailored to your specific dietary requirements and tastes.

In creating this book, I wanted to offer more than just recipes; I aimed to provide a guide that makes cooking a joyous and stress-free experience. So, if you are ready, I invite you to embrace this journey with an open heart and a hungry stomach. Let's turn up the heat and get frying!!

vegetarian   vegan   gluten-free   Spicy

We hope you've enjoyed exploring the flavorful world of our cookbook. We'd be grateful for your review on Amazon. Your reviews are not just comments; they are the guiding stars for others who seek similar culinary experiences and for us as we continue to create.

It will take only a few minutes to share your thoughts:

1. Log into your Amazon account.
2. Go to "Accounts & Lists" => "Your Orders."
3. Find our cookbook and select "Write a Product Review".

Thank you for your support, and happy cooking!

Bonus

To further support your transition to a low-sodium lifestyle, we've included a special bonus that aligns perfectly with your health-conscious journey. By scanning the QR code below, you'll gain access to two fantastic resources: "Low Sodium Smoothies," – a set of deliciously healthy smoothie recipes, and "A Guide to Reading Food Labels for Low Sodium Choices."

Both of these resources aim to enhance your culinary experience, enabling you to enjoy healthful, flavorful meals without any compromises. Scan the code now to access these resources instantly:

Prep. Time: 10 min   Cook Time: 15 min   Service: 4

Chicken and Veggie Enchiladas

Ingredients:

- 4 large whole wheat tortillas
- 2 chicken breasts
- 1 cup low-sodium black beans, drained, rinsed
- 1 bell pepper, thinly sliced
- 1 onion, thinly sliced
- 1 cup low-sodium enchilada sauce
- 1/2 cup low-fat shredded cheese
- 1 teaspoon ground cumin
- 1 teaspoon chili powder
- 1 teaspoon garlic powder
- Fresh lettuce for serving
- 1/4 cup light sour cream
- Fresh cilantro for garnish

Directions:

1. Shred the raw chicken breasts and toss the shreds with cumin, chili powder, and garlic powder.
2. Preheat your air fryer to 360° (182°C). Place the seasoned shredded chicken in the air fryer basket. Cook it for 10 minutes. The chicken should be fully cooked and get a bit crispy on the edges.
3. Once the chicken is cooked, take it out and mix it in a bowl with black beans, chopped bell pepper, and onion.
4. Spread the tortillas and evenly distribute the chicken mixture onto each one. Roll the tortillas up tightly, then place them seam-side down in the air fryer basket. Pour enchilada sauce over the top and then finish with a generous sprinkle of cheese.
5. Air fry the enchiladas at the same temperature for another 5minutes.
6. Serve the enchiladas laid on a bed of fresh lettuce. Add a dollop of light sour cream on top and garnish with some fresh cilantro for the perfect finish.

Nutrition information (per serving):

Calories: 370 kcal | Sodium: 320 mg |
Cholesterol: 80 mg | Protein: 30 g| Fat: 10 g |
Carbohydrates: 38 g

Notes:

Prep. Time: 8 min   Cook Time: 14 min   Service: 4

Broccoli and Corn Fritters

Ingredients:

- 2 cups broccoli florets
- 1/2 cup corn kernels (thawed if frozen)
- 1/4 cup onion, finely chopped
- 1/2 cup almond flour
- 2 large egg
- 1/2 teaspoon garlic powder
- 1/2 teaspoon paprika
- Freshly ground black pepper, to taste
- Olive oil spray

Directions:

1. Steam the broccoli florets until just tender, about 3-4 minutes, then chop finely.
2. combine the chopped broccoli with corn kernels, onion, egg, garlic powder, paprika, and black pepper in a bowl. Mix well to form a batter.
3. Preheat the air fryer to 390°F (199°C) and spray the air fryer basket with olive oil.
4. Shape the mixture into small patties, gently dip each in almond flour, and place them in the air fryer basket. Ensure they are not touching so the air can circulate freely.
5. Air fry for 8 minutes, flipping halfway through until crisp.
6. Serve the fritters warm.

Nutrition information (per serving):

Calories: 506 | Sodium: 65mg | Cholesterol: 47mg | Protein: 16g | Fat:7g | Carbohydrates: 9g

Notes:

Herbed Scotch Eggs

Ingredients:

- 4 large eggs
- 1 pound lean ground turkey
- 1 teaspoon dried parsley
- 1 teaspoon dried thyme
- 1/2 teaspoon garlic powder
- 1/2 teaspoon onion powder
- 1/4 teaspoon black pepper
- 1/4 cup almond flour
- Olive oil spray

Directions:

1. Start by hard-boiling the eggs: place the eggs in a saucepan, cover with water, bring to a boil, then cover and remove from heat. Let them sit for 5-9 minutes (depending on how solid the center you prefer). Remove the eggs, cool them in ice water, and peel.
2. Combine the ground turkey or chicken with thyme, parsley, garlic powder, onion powder, and black pepper. Divide the mixture into four equal portions.
3. Flatten each portion of the meat mixture and wrap it around each egg, fully encasing the egg. Roll the meat-coated eggs in almond flour for a light breading.
4. Preheat the air fryer to 390°F (199°C). Spray the air fryer basket with olive oil spray.
5. Place the Scotch eggs in the basket and air fry for 15 minutes, turning halfway through, or until the meat is thoroughly cooked and has a golden exterior.
6. Serve warm.

Nutrition information (per serving):
Calories: 250 kcal | Sodium: 120 mg | Cholesterol: 215 mg | Protein: 29g | Fat: 13 g | Carbohydrates: 2 g

Notes:

Prep. Time: 13 min   Cook Time: 8 min   Service: 4

Shrimp and White Bean Bruschetta

Ingredients:

- 4 slices of whole-grain bread
- 1 cup cooked white cannellini beans, rinsed and low-sodium
- 12 large shrimp, peeled and deveined
- 1/4 cup grated Parmesan cheese
- 4 cups mixed greens
- 3 tablespoons olive oil
- 1 garlic clove, minced
- 1 teaspoon dried oregano
- 1 tablespoon balsamic vinegar
- 1 teaspoon Dijon mustard
- Black pepper to taste
- Fresh parsley, chopped for garnish

Directions:

1. Preheat the air fryer to 360°F(182°C). Toss the shrimp with olive oil and black pepper, then place them in the air fryer basket. Cook for 4 minutes or until pink and cooked through.
2. Once the shrimp are ready, remove them and set them aside. Place the slices of bread in the air fryer and cook for 2 minutes until lightly toasted.
3. In a bowl, mix the white beans with minced garlic, oregano, and black pepper. Set aside.
4. Assemble the bruschetta by spooning the white bean mixture onto each slice of toast, topping with three shrimp per slice, and sprinkling with Parmesan cheese.
5. To make the salad, whisk together balsamic vinegar, Dijon mustard, and olive oil. Toss the dressing with the mixed greens.
6. Serve the bruschetta alongside the green salad and garnish with fresh parsley.

Nutrition information (per serving):

Calories: 350 | Sodium: 150mg | Cholesterol: 45mg | Protein: 15g | Fat:10g | Carbohydrates: 22g

Notes:

Prep. Time: 16 min   Cook Time: 30 min   Service: 4

Hasselback Potatoes with Colorful Salad

Ingredients:

- 4 medium potatoes, washed and patted dry
- 1 tablespoon olive oil
- 1 zucchini, sliced into half-moons
- 1 red bell pepper, sliced
- 1 cup frozen corn kernels, defrost
- 4 cups mixed salad greens
- 1 lemon, cut into wedges
- Fresh dill, chopped, for garnish
- Black pepper, to taste

Directions:

1. Carefully slice each potato crosswise at 1/8 inch intervals, avoiding cutting all the way through.
2. Preheat the air fryer to 360°F(182°C). Brush the potatoes with olive oil and place them in the air fryer basket. Cook for 30 minutes or until they're crispy on the outside and tender inside. When there are about 10 minutes left, add the zucchini and red bell pepper to the basket with the potatoes so they can cook together.
3. Arrange the mixed salad greens on a plate. Once the potatoes and vegetables are done, place them atop the greens.
4. Squeeze fresh lemon juice over the salad for added zest and sprinkle with fresh dill and a bit of black pepper for extra flavor.
5. Serve this dish while the potatoes are still warm for the best experience.

Nutrition information (per serving):
Calories: 200 | Sodium: 70mg | Cholesterol: 0mg | Protein: 5g | Fat: 4g| Carbohydrates: 40g

Notes:

Prep. Time: 15 min   Cook Time: 20 min   Service: 4

Herbed Turkey Cutlets with Salad

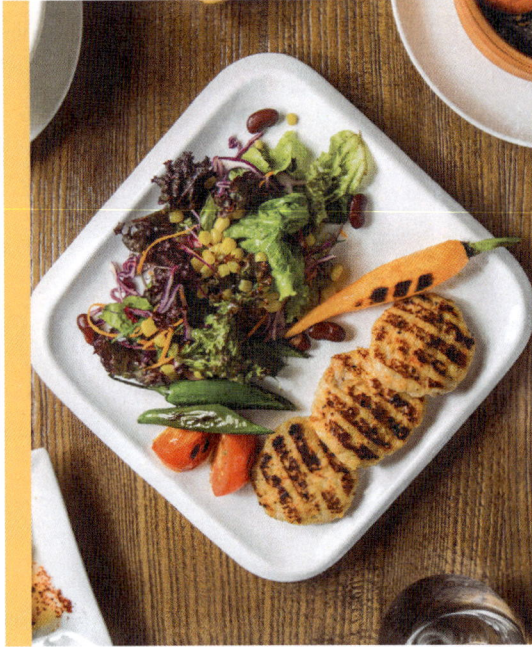

Ingredients:

- 1 pound ground turkey
- 1 tablespoon olive oil
- 1 teaspoon dried thyme
- 1 teaspoon dried oregano
- 1/2 teaspoon garlic powder
- 1/4 teaspoon black pepper
- Fresh lemon juice(from 1/2 a lemon)
- 4 cups mixed greens
- 1/2 cup cherry tomatoes, halved
- 1/4 cup shredded purple cabbage
- 1/4 cup shredded carrots
- 1/4 cup corn kernels
- 1/4 cup kidney beans, rinsed and drained
- 1 small cucumber, sliced
- 2 tablespoons balsamic vinegar (for dressing)
- 1 tablespoon olive oil(for dressing)

Directions:

1. Preheat your air fryer to 360°F(182°C).
2. Next, in a small bowl, combine the ground turkey, olive oil, thyme, oregano, garlic powder, and black pepper.
3. Shape the seasoned turkey into patties and place them in the air fryer. Cook for 10 minutes, flip them, and then cook for another 10 minutes.
4. While the turkey cooks, prepare a salad by tossing mixed greens, tomatoes, cabbage, carrots, corn, kidney beans, and cucumber.
5. For the dressing, whisk balsamic vinegar and olive oil and drizzle over the salad, tossing to combine.
6. Serve the air-fried turkey patties with the fresh garden salad.

Nutrition information (per serving):
Calories: 250 | Sodium: 70 mg | Cholesterol: 50 mg | Protein: 29 g |Fat: 10 g | Carbohydrates: 12 g

Notes:

Prep. Time: 15 min   Cook Time: 15 min   Service: 4

Golden Potato Pancakes

Ingredients:

- 4 large russet potatoes, peeled
- 1 small onion, finely chopped
- 2 cloves of garlic, minced
- 1/4 cup almond flour
- 1 large egg
- 1/2 teaspoon black pepper
- 1/2 teaspoon paprika
- Fresh parsley for garnish

Directions:

1. Grate the potatoes and then wring out all the moisture using a clean kitchen towel.
2. In a big bowl, mix the dried grated potatoes with onion, garlic, almond flour, egg, black pepper, and paprika until everything is well combined.
3. Shape this mixture into small, 1/2-inch thick patties.
4. Preheat your air fryer to 380°F(193°C). Arrange the potato pancakes in the air fryer basket in a single layer, making sure they're not touching.
5. Air fry the pancakes for 15 minutes, flipping them halfway through until they are golden brown and have a crispy texture.
6. Finish by garnishing with fresh parsley before serving.

Nutrition information (per serving):
Calories: 210 | Sodium: 20 mg | Cholesterol: 0 mg | Protein: 4 g | Fat:2 g | Carbohydrates: 44 g

Notes:

Prep. Time: 9 min   Cook Time: 15 min   Service: 4

Fluffy Banana Berry Pancakes

Ingredients:

- 1 cup all-purpose flour
- 1 tablespoon sodium-free baking powder
- 1 tablespoon sugar
- 1 cup low-fat milk
- 1 egg
- 1 ripe banana, mashed
- ½ cup mixed berries (raspberries, blueberries, etc.)
- 1 teaspoon vanilla extract
- Cooking spray

Directions:

1. Mixed together flour, baking powder, and sugar in a large bowl.
2. Next, in a separate bowl, beat together egg, milk, mashed banana, and vanilla extract until it's all nicely blended.
3. Pour the wet mixture into the dry ingredients and stir until combined. Then, gently fold in the berries.
4. Preheat your air fryer to 360°F (182°C). Spray the air fryer basket with cooking spray to keep the pancakes from sticking.
5. Carefully spoon the batter into the air fryer, forming small round sand leaving some space between each pancake.
6. Cook them for about 7-8 minutes until they turn golden brown and are cooked through, flipping them once halfway through.
7. Serve your pancakes with a sweet drizzle of honey and top them with extra fresh berries.

Nutrition information (per serving):
Calories: 210 | Sodium: 95 mg | Cholesterol: 48mg | Protein: 6g | Fat:2g | Carbohydrates: 41g

Notes:

Prep. Time: 15 min   Cook Time: 15 min   Service: 4

French Breakfast

Ingredients:

- 1 package of ready-to-bake low-sodium croissant dough
- 1/4 cup almond paste
- 1 tablespoon unsalted butter, melted
- 1 tablespoon honey
- 1/4 cup sliced almonds
- 1 egg

Directions:

1. Preheat the air fryer to 360°F (182°C).
2. Unroll the croissant dough and separate it into triangles along the perforated lines.
3. On each dough triangle, spread a thin layer of almond paste. Begin rolling up each triangle from the wider end to form the classic croissant shape.
4. In a small bowl, lightly beat an egg and gently brush the croissants' tops with this mixture.
5. Place the croissants in the air fryer basket, spacing them out so they don't touch each other.
6. Air fry the croissants for about 12-15 minutes. You're looking for them to turn a lovely golden brown and puff up nicely.
7. Once done, brush the croissants with melted butter and honey for a glossy mixture.
8. Serve the croissants warm.

Nutrition information (per serving):
Calories: 350 | Sodium: 200mg | Cholesterol: 40mg | Protein: 8g | Fat:18g | Carbohydrates: 38g

Notes:

| Prep. Time: 10 min | Cook Time: 8 min | Service: 4 |

Cheese Blintzes

Ingredients:

- 1 cup all-purpose flour
- 2 large eggs
- 1,5 cup low-fat cottage cheese
- 1 tablespoon granulated sugar
- 1 teaspoon vanilla extract
- Cooking spray for air fryer
- Fresh blueberries for serving
- Greek yogurt for serving
- Fresh mint leaves for garnish

Directions:

1. Combine cottage cheese, eggs, and sugar in a mixing bowl and stir them together until they're nicely blended.
2. Form the mixture into small balls, then flatten them slightly to create patties. Coat each patty in flour, covering both sides, and then tap off any extra flour.
3. Preheat the air fryer to 350°F(177°C). Coat the air fryer basket with cooking spray. Carefully place the patties into the air fryer, spaced out so they have room to puff up a little.
4. Air fry them for 4 minutes, then turn them over gently and cook for another 4 minutes. They should be golden brown and fully cooked when done.
5. Serve warm with blueberries and a dollop of Greek yogurt. Add a few mint leaves for a fresh garnish.

Nutrition information (per serving):

Calories: 220 | Sodium: 125mg | Cholesterol: 96mg | Protein: 10g | Fat:5g | Carbohydrates: 30g

Notes:

Prep. Time: 7 min   Cook Time: 20 min   Service: 4

Garden Fresh Frittata

Ingredients:

- 6 large eggs
- 1/4 cup low-sodium milk
- 1/2 cup fresh spinach, chopped
- 1/2 cup cherry tomatoes, halved
- 1/4 cup feta cheese, crumbled
- 1 tablespoon olive oil
- 1/4 teaspoon black pepper
- 1/4 teaspoon garlic powder
- Fresh basil leaves for garnish

Directions:

1. Whisk together the eggs, milk, black pepper, and garlic powder.
2. Gently fold the spinach, tomatoes, and feta cheese into the egg mixture, combining them well.
3. Grease the air fryer basket with olive oil to prevent sticking.
4. Preheat the air fryer to 360°F(182°C). Pour the egg mixture into the air fryer basket.
5. Let the frittata cook for about 20 minutes or until it's fully cooked and has a light golden color on top.
6. Allow to cool for a few minutes before slicing. Garnish with fresh basil leaves before serving.

Nutrition information (per serving):

Calories: 180 | Sodium: 200 mg | Cholesterol: 280 mg| Protein: 12 g | Fat:12 g | Carbohydrates: 3 g

Notes:

Prep. Time: 12 min   Cook Time: 15 min   Service: 4

Mediterranean Chickpea Veggie Bowl

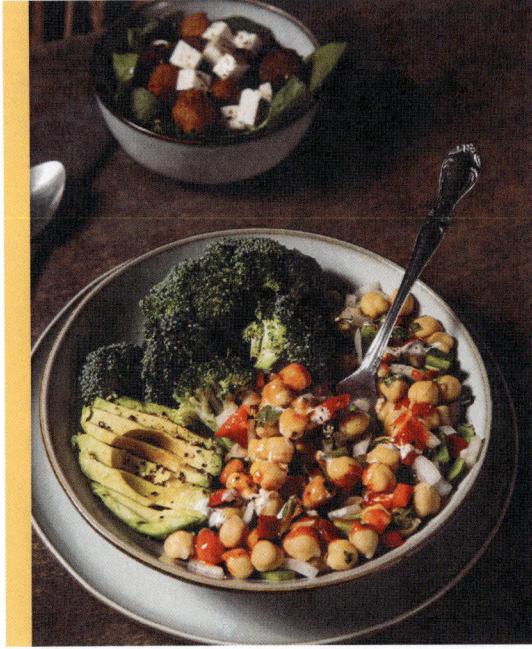

Ingredients:

- 2 cups chickpeas, drained and rinsed (low-sodium canned)
- 1 head of broccoli, cut into florets
- 1 ripe avocado, sliced
- 1 cup cherry tomatoes, halved
- 1 block of firm tofu, pressed and cubed
- 1 teaspoon garlic powder
- 2 tablespoons olive oil
- 1 teaspoon onion powder
- 1/2 teaspoon paprika
- 1/2 teaspoon ground black pepper
- 1/4 cup fresh parsley, finely chopped
- Lemon wedges for serving

Directions:

1. Preheat the air fryer to 380°F(193°C).
2. In a bowl, toss the chickpeas and tofu with olive oil, garlic powder, onion powder, paprika, and black pepper.
3. Place the chickpeas and tofu in the air fryer basket in a single layer. Cook for 10 minutes, shaking halfway through.
4. Add the broccoli florets to the basket in the last 5 minutes of cooking. Once done, let it cool slightly.
5. Assemble the bowls by dividing the air-fried chickpeas, tofu, and broccoli between four bowls. Add fresh avocado slices and cherry tomatoes to each bowl.
6. Serve with a lemon wedge on the side and garnish with fresh parsley.

Nutrition information (per serving):
Calories: 350 | Sodium: 100 mg | Cholesterol: 0 mg | Protein: 18 g | Fat:20 g | Carbohydrates: 30 g

Notes:

Prep. Time: 10 min | Cook Time: 11 min | Service: 4

Spicy Shrimp with Rice Noodles

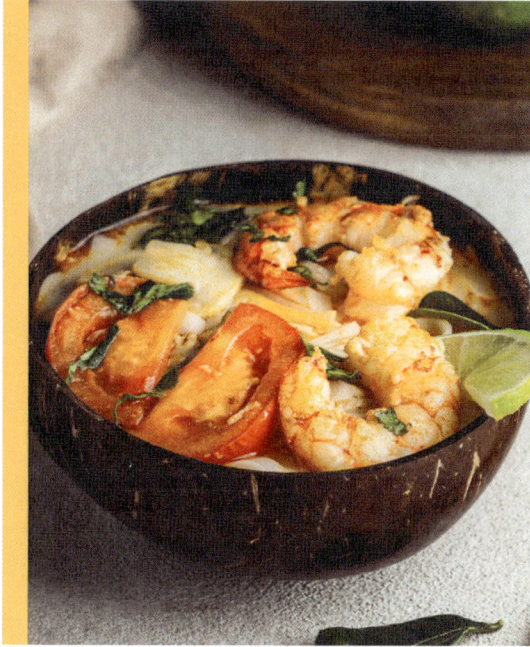

Ingredients:

- 1 pound large shrimp, peeled and deveined
- 8 ounces rice noodles
- 1 teaspoon olive oil
- 1 clove garlic, minced
- 1 teaspoon ginger, freshly grated
- 1/2 teaspoon red pepper flakes
- 2 large tomatoes, cut into wedges
- 2 cups baby spinach leaves
- 1 lime, cut into wedges
- 1 tablespoon low-sodium soy sauce
- 1 teaspoon honey
- Sesame seeds for garnish

Directions:

1. Preheat your air fryer to 400°F(204°C).
2. Toss the shrimp with olive oil, garlic, ginger, and red pepper flakes.
3. Place the shrimp in the air fryer basket. Cook for 6-9 minutes, flipping halfway through, until they are pink and slightly crispy.
4. While the shrimp is cooking, prepare the rice noodles according to the package instructions, aiming for al dente. Drain and keep warm.
5. In the last minute of cooking the shrimp, brush them with a low-sodium soy sauce and honey.
6. Assemble the noodle bowls by dividing the rice noodles into bowls. Top with air-fried shrimp, tomato wedges, and baby spinach leaves.
7. Serve accompanied by lime wedges for squeezing over the top and a sprinkle of sesame seeds.

Nutrition information (per serving):
Calories: 350 | Sodium: 200mg | Cholesterol: 120mg | Protein: 25g | Fat:5g | Carbohydrates: 48g

Notes:

Prep. Time: 12 min	Cook Time: 25 min	Service: 4

Beef Steak with Mushroom Sauce

Ingredients:

- 4 beef steaks (such as sirloin or ribeye), about 1-inch thick
- 1 pound baby potatoes, halved
- 1 tablespoon olive oil
- 1 teaspoon dried rosemary
- 1 teaspoon dried thyme
- Black pepper to taste
- 1/2 pound mushrooms, sliced
- 1 cup low-sodium beef broth
- 1 teaspoon cornstarch
- 1 garlic clove, minced
- 1 small onion, finely diced
- Fresh rosemary for garnish

Directions:

1. Toss the potatoes with half the olive oil, dried rosemary, thyme, and black pepper.
2. Preheat the air fryer to 400°F (204°C). Place the potatoes in the air fryer basket. Cook for 15 minutes.
3. While potatoes are cooking, season the beef steaks with black pepper and a touch of rosemary and thyme.
4. After the potatoes have cooked, move them to one side of the basket. Place the steaks in the basket and cook for another 10 minutes for medium-rare or until desired doneness.
5. For the mushroom sauce, warm up the rest of the olive oil in a saucepan on medium heat. Sauté the onion and garlic until they become translucent. Then, add the mushrooms and cook until they are nicely browned.
6. Puree the mushroom mixture until smooth, then pour it back into the saucepan. Dissolve the cornstarch in a little cold water and add it along with the beef broth to the saucepan. Heat until it simmers, then mix in the cornstarch solution and cook until the sauce thickens.
7. Serve the steak and potatoes with the mushroom sauce and garnish with fresh rosemary.

Nutrition information (per serving):
Calories: 500 | Sodium: 150mg | Cholesterol: 70mg | Protein: 30g | Fat:30g | Carbohydrates: 20g

Notes:

| Prep. Time: 10 min | Cook Time: 15 min | Service: 4 |

Chickpea Tomato Stew

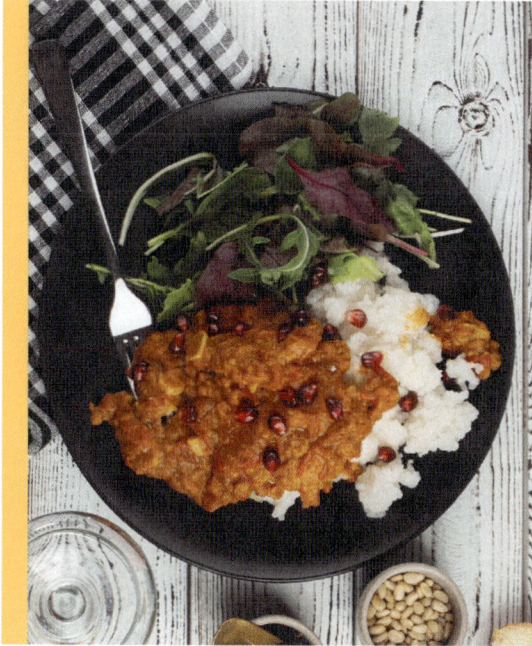

Ingredients:

- 2 cans (15 oz each) chickpeas, rinsed and drained
- 2 cups no-salt-added crushed tomatoes
- 1 teaspoon dried oregano
- 1 teaspoon dried basil
- 1/2 teaspoon garlic powder
- 1/2 teaspoon onion powder
- 1/4 teaspoon black pepper
- 1/4 teaspoon chili flakes
- 2 cups cooked brown rice
- 4 cups mixed greens
- 1/4 cup pomegranate seeds for garnish
- Olive oil spray

Directions:

1. Preheat the air fryer to 375°F (191°C).
2. Toss the chickpeas with olive oil spray, garlic powder, onion powder, oregano, basil, black pepper, and chili flakes.
3. Spread the chickpeas in the air fryer basket in a single layer. Air fry for 10-12 minutes until golden and slightly crispy, shaking the basket halfway through.
4. While the chickpeas are cooking, heat the crushed tomatoes in a saucepan over medium heat.
5. Next, add the cooked chickpeas to the saucepan once air-fried, and let simmer for 5 minutes to combine the flavors.
6. Prepare the herb rice by mixing the cooked brown rice with fresh or dried parsley and thyme to taste.
7. Assemble the salad with mixed greens and sprinkle pomegranate seeds on top.

Nutrition information (per serving):

Calories: 320 | Sodium: 180 mg | Cholesterol: 0mg | Protein: 10g | Fat: 5g | Carbohydrates: 60g

Notes:

Prep. Time: 16 min	Cook Time: 15 min	Service: 4

Savory Stuffed Bell Peppers

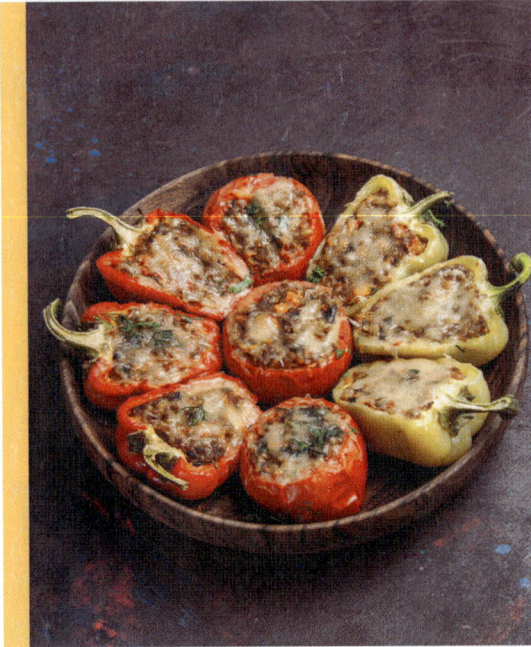

Ingredients:

- 4 large bell peppers, tops cut off and seeded
- 1 cup brown rice, cooked
- 1/2 pound ground turkey breast
- 1 cup diced tomatoes, no salt added
- 1/2 cup shredded mozzarella, low sodium
- 1/4 cup fresh parsley, chopped
- 1 teaspoon garlic powder
- 1 teaspoon onion powder
- 1/2 teaspoon black pepper
- Olive oil spray

Directions:

1. Preheat the Air Fryer to 350°F (175°C).
2. In a bowl, mix the cooked brown rice, ground turkey, diced tomatoes, garlic powder, onion powder, and black pepper. Stuff each bell pepper with the turkey and rice mixture.
3. Lightly spray the outside of the peppers with olive oil spray. Place the stuffed peppers into the Air Fryer basket.
4. Cook them for 15 minutes or until the peppers are tender.
5. In the last 2 minutes of cooking, sprinkle the tops with mozzarella and continue to cook until the cheese is slightly golden.
6. Garnish with fresh parsley before serving.

Nutrition information (per serving):
Calories: 300 | Sodium: 150 mg | Cholesterol: 50 mg | Protein: 26 g | Fat: 9 g | Carbohydrates: 30 g

Notes:

Prep. Time: 5 min   Cook Time: 10 min   Service: 4

Lemon-Dill Salmon with Green Beans

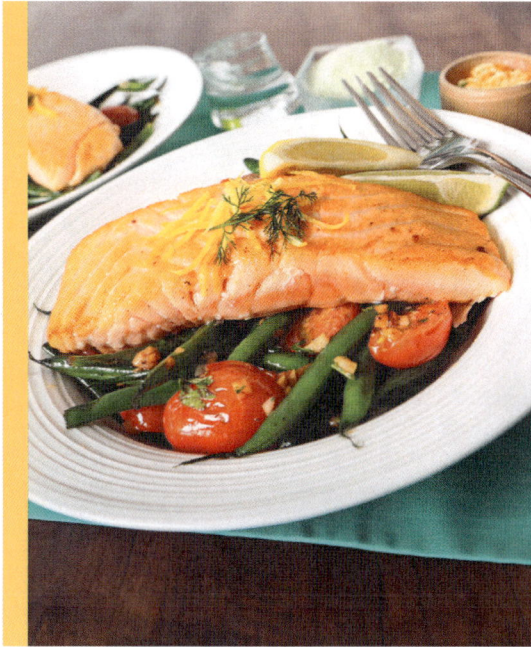

Ingredients:

- 4 salmon fillets (4-6oz each)
- 2 cups fresh green beans, ends trimmed
- 1 cup cherry tomatoes, halved
- 2 tablespoons olive oil
- 1 lemon, zest and juice
- 2 tablespoons fresh dill, chopped
- Freshly ground black pepper, to taste

Directions:

1. Preheat the Air Fryer to 380°F(193°C).
2. Toss the cherry tomatoes and green beans with 1 tablespoon of olive oil and black pepper.
3. Place the green bean mixture in the Air Fryer basket and cook for 4minutes. Set aside.
4. Dry the salmon fillets thoroughly with paper towels. Then, brush each fillet with the leftover olive oil and season them with lemon zest and a dash of black pepper for flavor.
5. Place the salmon fillets in the basket. Cook for 7 -10 minutes.
6. Dish out the salmon and green beans, adding a drizzle of lemon juice and a sprinkling of fresh dill for garnish.

Nutrition information (per serving):
Calories: 300 | Sodium: 70 mg | Cholesterol: 55 mg | Protein: 23 g |Fat: 18 g | Carbohydrates: 6 g

Notes:

| Prep. Time: 12 min | Cook Time: 25 min | Service: 4 |

Herb-Crusted Ribs with Potatoes

Ingredients:

- 8 pork ribs
- 1 pound baby potatoes, quartered
- 2 tablespoons olive oil
- 1 teaspoon dried rosemary
- 1 teaspoon dried thyme
- 1 teaspoon dried oregano
- Black pepper to taste
- 1 garlic clove, minced
- Fresh parsley, chopped for garnish
- Sesame seeds for garnish

Directions:

1. Preheat the air fryer to 380°F (193°C).
2. Rub the ribs with half the olive oil, minced garlic, rosemary, thyme, oregano, and black pepper.
3. In a separate bowl, toss the potatoes with the remaining olive oil and the same herbs used for the ribs.
4. Place the ribs in the air fryer basket, cook for 20 minutes, and turn half way through.
5. When the ribs are halfway done, add the seasoned potatoes to the basket and continue to cook until the ribs are cooked through and the potatoes are tender and golden brown.
6. Serve the ribs and potatoes garnished with fresh parsley.

Nutrition information (per serving):
Calories: 500 | Sodium: 120mg | Cholesterol: 95mg | Protein: 25g | Fat:35g | Carbohydrates: 20g

Notes:

Prep. Time: 14 min   Cook Time: 15 min   Service: 4

Thai-Style Chicken Salad

Ingredients:

- 4 small, boneless, skinless chicken breasts
- 1 tablespoon olive oil
- 1 teaspoon ground ginger
- 1/4 teaspoon crushed red pepper flakes
- 4 cups mixed salad greens
- 1 cup shredded carrots
- 1/2 cup cherry tomatoes, halved
- 1/4 cup red cabbage, shredded
- 1/4 cup cashews, unsalted
- 1/2 cup pineapple chunks, fresh or canned in juice
- Fresh cilantro leaves for garnish

Directions:

1. Preheat the air fryer to 375°F (190°C).
2. Next, coat the chicken breasts with olive oil, then season with ground ginger and red pepper flakes.
3. Place chicken in the air fryer basket and cook for 15-18 minutes.
4. While the chicken is cooking, prepare the salad by tossing the mixed greens, shredded carrots, cherry tomatoes, red cabbage, and pineapple chunks ina large bowl.
5. Once the chicken is done, let it rest for 3 minutes before slicing it into strips.
6. Divide the salad mix among four plates, top with sliced chicken, sprinkle with cashews, and garnish with fresh cilantro leaves.

Nutrition information (per serving):
Calories: 320 | Sodium: 125mg | Cholesterol: 65mg | Protein: 28g | Fat:14g | Carbohydrates: 18g

Notes:

Prep. Time: 15 min   Cook Time: 10 min   Service: 4

Classic Beef Burgers

Ingredients:

- 1 pound lean ground beef (90% lean)
- 1 teaspoon garlic powder
- 1 teaspoon onion powder
- 1/2 teaspoon freshly ground black pepper
- 4 low-sodium whole wheat burger buns
- 4 lettuce leaves
- 1 tomato, sliced
- 4 slices low-sodium cheddar cheese
- 1/4 cup low sodium pickles, sliced
- 1 small red onion, thinly sliced

Directions:

1. In a bowl, combine ground beef, black pepper, and onion powder and mix well. Then, split the mixture into four equal parts and shape each one into a patty.
2. Preheat the Air Fryer to 360°F (182°C). Place the patties in the air fryer basket, ensuring they do not touch.
3. Let them cook for 10 minutes, flipping each burger once at the half way mark until they're cooked to your liking. In the final minute of cooking, add a slice of cheese on top of each burger patty to melt.
4. Assemble the burgers by placing a lettuce leaf on each bun's bottom, followed by the cooked patty, tomato slice, pickles, and red onion. Cap with the top bun.
5. Serve with a side salad.

Nutrition information (per serving):
Calories: 350 | Sodium: 300 mg | Cholesterol: 90 mg | Protein: 26 g | Fat:15 g | Carbohydrates: 27 g

Notes:

24

Prep. Time: 10 min   Cook Time: 8 min   Service: 4

Chicken and Corn Quesadillas

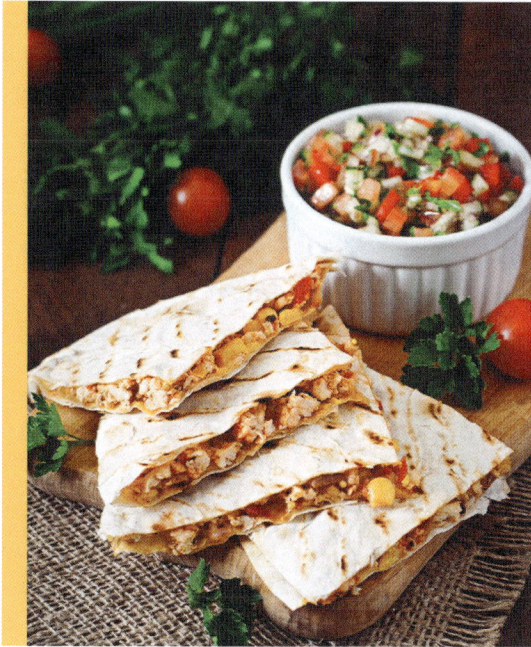

Ingredients:

- 4 large whole wheat tortillas
- 1 cup cooked and shredded chicken breast
- 1/2 cup sweet corn kernels, canned and drained or fresh
- 1/2 cup diced red bell pepper
- 1 cup shredded cheddar cheese, low-sodium
- 1 teaspoon cumin powder
- 1 teaspoon smoked paprika
- Olive oil spray
- Salsa for serving

Directions:

1. In a bowl, mix the shredded chicken with cumin and paprika.
2. Lay out the tortillas and evenly distribute the chicken, corn, bell pepper, and cheese among them on one half of each tortilla. Then, fold the other half over the fillings to form a half-moon shape.
3. Preheat the air fryer to 360°F (180°C). Lightly spray the outside of the quesadillas with olive oil spray and place them in the air fryer basket, ensuring they are not overlapping.
4. Cook for about 4 minutes on each side until the quesadillas are golden brown and the cheese is melted.
5. Cut into wedges and serve with salsa.

Nutrition information (per serving):
Calories: 350 | Sodium: 320 mg | Cholesterol: 60 mg | Protein: 25 g | Fat:15 g | Carbohydrates: 30 g

Notes:

Prep. Time: 12 min   Cook Time: 15 min   Service: 4

Teriyaki Tofu

Ingredients:

- 14 oz block extra-firm tofu, pressed and cut into cubes
- 2 tablespoons low-sodium teriyaki sauce
- 1 tablespoon rice vinegar
- 1 tablespoon water
- 1 tablespoon maple syrup
- 1 teaspoon garlic, minced
- 1 teaspoon ginger, minced
- 1 tablespoon cornstarch
- 1 teaspoon sesame seeds
- Green onions, chopped for garnish

Directions:

1. Press the tofu for 5 minutes to remove excess moisture, then cut into 1-inch cubes.
2. Create the teriyaki marinade by combining teriyaki sauce, rice vinegar, water, maple syrup, garlic, and ginger in a bowl.
3. Place tofu cubes in the marinade and ensure each piece is well coated. Allow it to sit for at least 5 minutes.
4. After marinating, drain the tofu, reserving the marinade. Toss the tofu with cornstarch to coat evenly.
5. Preheat the air fryer to 380°F (193°C). Arrange the tofu in the basket so it's in one layer. Cook it for 15 minutes, flipping it over half way through until it becomes crispy and takes on a golden color.
6. While the tofu is cooking, pour the reserved marinade into a small saucepan. Let it simmer and reduce down until it becomes a thick glaze.
7. Once the tofu is done, toss it in the thickened teriyaki glaze until evenly coated.
8. Finish by sprinkling sesame seeds and chopped green onions over the top as a garnish.

Nutrition information (per serving):
Calories: 160 | Sodium: 200 mg | Cholesterol: 0 mg | Protein: 12 g | Fat:6 g | Carbohydrates: 16 g

Notes:

26

Prep. Time: 16 min   Cook Time: 25 min   Service: 4

Herbed Turkey and Vegetable Medley

Ingredients:

- 1 pound turkey breast, cut into bite-sized pieces
- 1 medium red bell pepper, diced
- 1 medium green bell pepper, diced
- 2 medium tomatoes, diced
- 1 medium zucchini, diced
- 1 tablespoon olive oil
- 1 teaspoon dried thyme
- 1 teaspoon dried rosemary
- 1/2 teaspoon garlic powder
- 1/2 teaspoon onion powder
- 1/2 teaspoon cayenne pepper
- Freshly ground black pepper, to taste

Directions:

1. Preheat your air fryer to 360°F (182°C).
2. Pat the turkey pieces dry with paper towels.
3. In a bowl, combine the turkey with olive oil, thyme, rosemary, garlic powder, onion powder, cayenne pepper and black pepper. Toss to coat evenly.
4. Put the turkey in the air fryer basket and cook for 10-15 minutes. Shake the basket or stir the mixture halfway through to ensure even cooking.
5. Add the diced vegetables to the turkey and toss again to ensure everything is seasoned. Cook for an additional 10 minutes.
6. Serve the cooked turkey and vegetables hot from the air fryer.

Nutrition information (per serving):
Calories: 220 | Sodium: 70mg | Cholesterol: 55mg | Protein: 27g | Fat: 7g | Carbohydrates: 10g

Notes:

Prep. Time: 11 min   Cook Time: 8 min   Service: 4

Beef and Bean Tacos

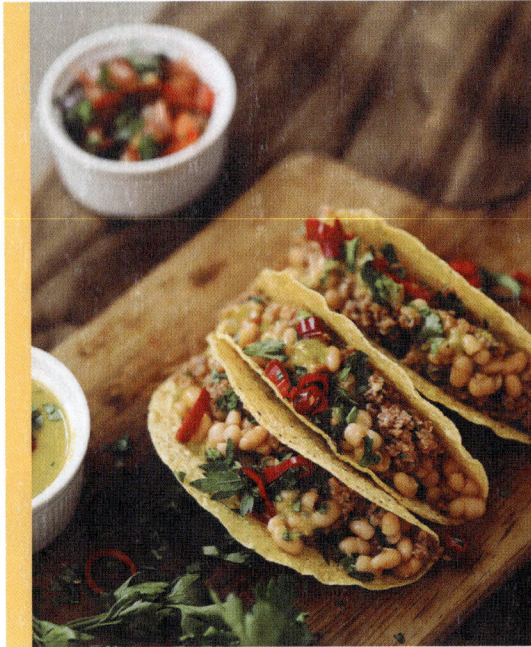

Ingredients:

- 8 corn tortillas
- 1 pound lean ground beef (90% lean)
- 1 cup cooked white beans, low sodium or no salt added
- 1 teaspoon ground cumin
- 1 teaspoon smoked paprika
- 1/2 teaspoon garlic powder
- 1/2 teaspoon onion powder
- 1/2 teaspoon black pepper
- 1/2 cup fresh salsa (pico de gallo)
- Fresh cilantro, chopped for garnish

Directions:

1. Preheat the air fryer to 380°F (193°C).
2. In a bowl, thoroughly mix the ground beef with cumin, smoked paprika, garlic powder, onion powder, and black pepper. Shape the beef mixture into small patties to fit into the taco shells.
3. Cook the patties in the Air Fryer basket for 6 minutes, flipping them half way through.
4. Warm the tortillas in the Air Fryer for about 2 minutes or until soft and warm.
5. Once the beef is fully cooked, use a fork to break it into chunks, then mix it with the cooked white beans.
6. Fill the tortillas with the beef and bean mixture. Top each taco with fresh salsa.

Nutrition information (per serving):
Calories: 320 | Sodium: 200 mg | Cholesterol: 60 mg | Protein: 26 g | Fat:9 g |Carbohydrates: 35g

Notes:

Prep. Time: 12 min   Cook Time: 40 min   Service: 4

Honey-Glazed Chicken with Vegetables

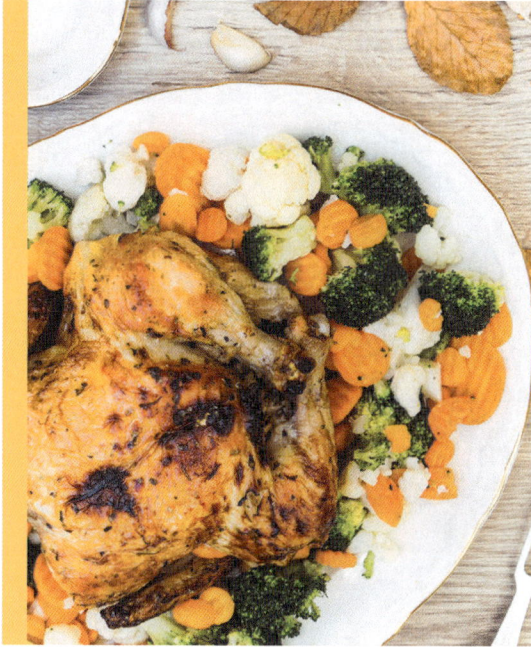

Ingredients:

- 1 whole chicken (approximately 3 pounds), skin removed
- 2 tablespoons olive oil
- 1/4 cup honey
- 1 teaspoon smoked paprika
- 1/2 teaspoon ground black pepper
- 2 cloves garlic, minced
- 1 lemon, zested and juiced
- 2 cups broccoli florets
- 2 cups cauliflower florets
- 1 cup carrots, sliced
- Olive oil spray
- 1 teaspoon onion powder
- 1 teaspoon garlic powder

Directions:

1. Pat the chicken dry with paper towels. Next, combine olive oil, honey, lemon zest and, juice, smoked paprika, pepper, and minced garlic to create a glaze.
2. Rub the glaze evenly over the chicken. Let it rest for 20 minutes at room temperature to allow the flavors to infuse.
3. Preheat your air fryer to 360°F (182°C). Place the chicken in the air fryer basket and cook for 30 minutes.
4. While the chicken cooks, toss the broccoli, cauliflower, and carrots with onion powder, garlic powder, and a light spray of olive oil.
5. After 30 minutes, carefully remove the basket and add the vegetables around the chicken. Cook for an additional 10 minutes, or until the chicken's internal temperature reaches 165°F (74°C) and the vegetables are tender.
6. Once done, remove the chicken and vegetables from the air fryer. Let the chicken rest for 5 minutes before carving.
7. Serve the carved chicken with a generous helping of the roasted vegetables.

Nutrition information (per serving):

Calories: 360 | Sodium: 80mg | Cholesterol: 90mg | Protein: 27g | Fat:15g | Carbohydrates: 18g

Notes:

Prep. Time: 13 min   Cook Time: 25 min   Service: 4

Lemon-Herb Turkey and Vegetables

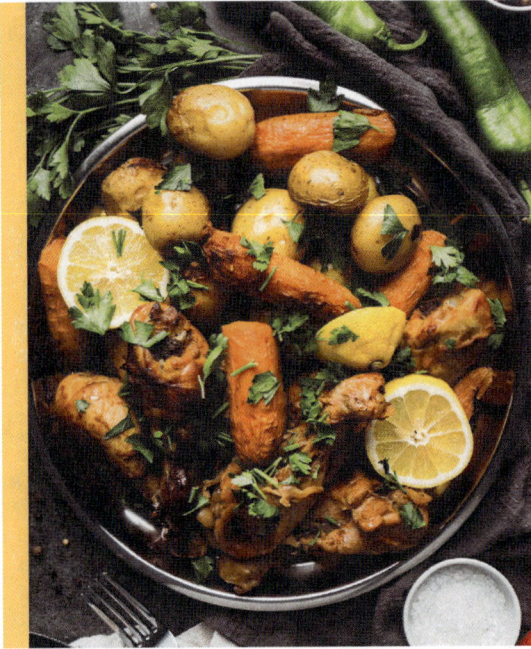

Ingredients:

- 4 turkey cutlets (about 1/2 inch thick)
- 1 lemon, one half juiced and the other half cut into slices
- 2 tablespoons olive oil
- 1 teaspoon dried thyme
- 1 teaspoon dried rosemary
- 1/2 teaspoon black pepper
- 2 large carrots, cut into sticks
- 8 small new potatoes, halved
- Fresh parsley, chopped for garnish

Directions:

1. combine lemon juice, olive oil, thyme, rosemary, and black pepper to create a marinade.
2. Place the turkey cutlets in the marinade, ensuring they are well coated. Allow them to marinate in the refrigerator for at least 30 minutes.
3. Preheat the air fryer to 380°F (193°C).
4. Remove the turkey from the marinade and place the cutlets in the air fryer basket. Air fry them for 10 minutes.
5. After 10 minutes, add the carrots and potatoes to the basket with the turkey cutlets. Distribute the lemon slices over the turkey and vegetables.
6. Continue air frying for another 15 minutes or until the turkey is cooked through and the vegetables are tender.
7. Garnish with chopped fresh parsley.

Nutrition information (per serving):
Calories: 300 | Sodium: 70mg | Cholesterol: 55mg | Protein: 27g | Fat:9g | Carbohydrates: 22g

Notes:

Prep. Time: 10 min   Cook Time: 12 min   Service: 4

Beef Steak with Garden Salad

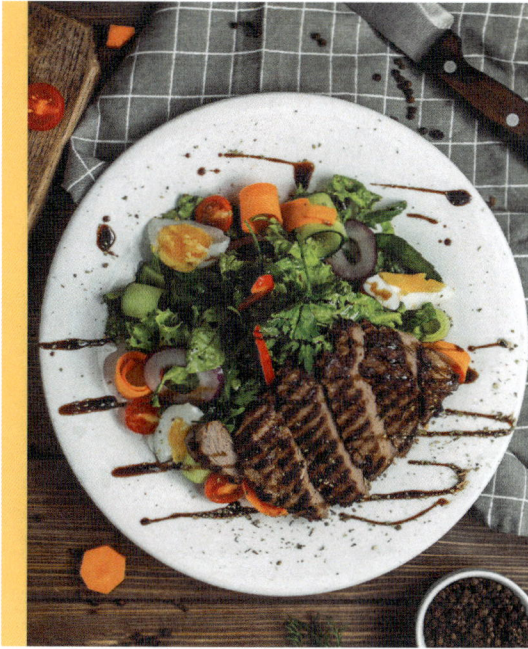

Ingredients:

- 4 beef steaks (around 6 ounces each), trimmed of excess fat
- 3 teaspoons olive oil
- 1 teaspoon garlic powder
- 1 teaspoon onion powder
- 1 teaspoon dried thyme
- 1 teaspoon dried rosemary
- 1/2 teaspoon black pepper
- 8 cups mixed salad greens
- 1 cup cherry tomatoes, halved
- 1 medium cucumber, sliced
- 4 hard-boiled eggs, sliced
- 1/4 cup red onion, thinly sliced
- 1/4 cup balsamic vinegar
- 1/2 teaspoon dried oregano

Directions:

1. Preheat your air fryer to 400°F (200°C).
2. Rub each steak with 2 teaspoons of olive oil in total, ensuring each piece is lightly coated. Season the steaks evenly with onion powder, garlic powder, dried thyme, black pepper, and dried rosemary.
3. Place the steaks in the air fryer basket, making sure they don't overlap. Cook the steaks for about 6 minutes on each side for medium-rare or until your desired doneness is reached.
4. While the steaks are cooking, in a large bowl, assemble the salad by combining the mixed greens, cucumber slices, cherry tomatoes, and red onion slices.
5. In a small bowl, whisk together balsamic vinegar, olive oil, and dried oregano to create the dressing. Next, pour the dressing over the salad, tossing it so everything gets evenly coated. Add freshly ground black pepper to the salad according to your taste.
6. Once the steaks are done, allow them to rest for a few minutes befo re slicing.
7. Serve the steaks alongside the garden salad.

Nutrition information (per serving):

Calories: 350 | Sodium: 120mg | Cholesterol: 105mg | Protein:38g | Fat: 17g | Carbohydrates: 8g

Notes:

Prep. Time: 12 min	Cook Time: 10 min	Service: 4

Sea Bass with Herb Pesto

Ingredients:

- 4 sea bass fillets (about 6 ounces each)
- 2 tablespoons olive oil
- Freshly ground black pepper, to taste
- 1 cup mixed salad greens
- 1/2 cup cherry tomatoes, halved
- 1/2 cup radishes, thinly sliced
- 1 lemon, cut into wedges
- 2 tablespoons homemade orstore-bought low-sodium pesto

Directions:

1. Brush the sea bass fillets with olive oil and season with black pepper.
2. Preheat the air fryer to 360°F (182°C). Place the fillets in the air fryer basket, ensuring they don't overlap, even when cooking. Cook for 10minutes or until the fish flakes have a golden exterior.
3. While the fish is cooking, toss the salad greens, cherry tomatoes, and radishes together.
4. Once cooked, transfer the sea bass to plates, top with a dollop of pesto, and serve alongside the fresh salad and lemon wedges.

Nutrition information (per serving):

Calories: 280 | Sodium: 70mg | Cholesterol: 60mg | Protein: 23g | Fat:18g | Carbohydrates: 3g

Notes:

Prep. Time: 15 min   Cook Time: 30 min   Service: 4

Crispy Chicken Cutlets

Ingredients:

- 4 boneless, skinless chicken breasts
- 1/2 cup unsalted almond flour
- 2 large eggs, beaten
- 1 cup panko breadcrumbs
- 1 teaspoon garlic powder
- 1 teaspoon onion powder
- 1/2 teaspoon paprika
- Olive oil spray
- 2 large potatoes, cut into cubes
- 1 medium green bell pepper, sliced
- 1 large tomato, sliced
- 1/2 cup pomegranate seeds
- 4 lettuce leaves for garnish
- 1 long green chili for garnish

Directions:

1. Begin by prepping the chicken cutlets: place them between two sheets of parchment paper and pound them until they reach an even thickness of about1/2 inch.
2. Prepare a breading station with three shallow dishes: one with almond flour, one with beaten eggs, and one with panko breadcrumbs mixed with garlic powder, onion powder, and paprika.
3. Dip each chicken breast first into the almond flour, then the egg, and finally coat with the seasoned breadcrumbs.
4. Preheat the air fryer to 375°F (190°C). Place the breaded chicken cutlets in the air fryer basket and spray lightly with olive oil. Air fry for15 minutes, flipping halfway through, until the chicken is golden and cooked through.
5. Meanwhile, toss the potato cubes with a light spray of olive oil and a pinch of paprika. After the chicken has cooked for 10 minutes, add the potatoes and air fryer for the remaining 20 minutes or until crispy and golden.
6. On a plate, lay out the sliced tomatoes and lettuce leaves. Scatter pomegranate seeds over them, and place the sliced green bell pepper on top. Adda long green chili for garnish and extra spiciness.

Nutrition information (per serving):
Calories: 410 | Sodium: 70 g | Cholesterol: 110mg | Protein: 28g | Fat:14g | Carbohydrates: 40g

Notes:

Prep. Time: 15 min   Cook Time: 20 min   Service: 4

Stuffed Eggplant

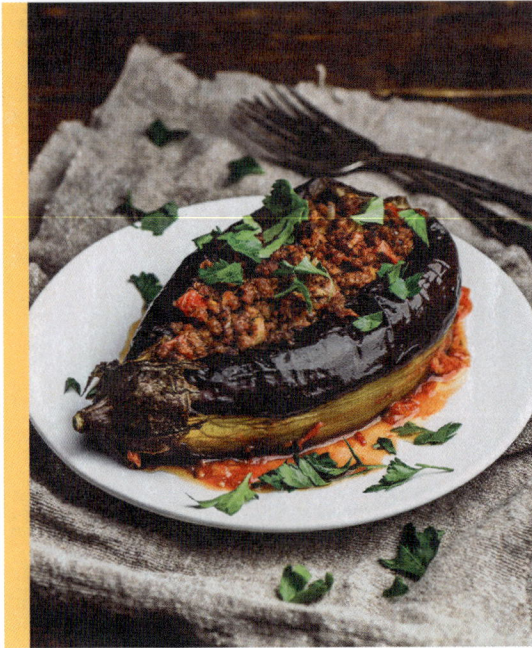

Ingredients:

- 2 large eggplants
- 1/2 lb ground lean beef
- 1/4 cup diced onions
- 1/2 cup diced bell peppers
- 2 cloves garlic, minced
- 1 cup chopped tomatoes
- 1 teaspoon dried oregano
- Fresh parsley, chopped, for garnish
- 1 tablespoon olive oil
- Freshly ground black pepper, to taste

Directions:

1. Cut the eggplants in half lengthwise and scoop out the middle to create boats, making sure to leave a sturdy border around the edges
 Brush each eggplant with olive oil and season with black pepper.
2. Mix the ground beef, onions, bell peppers, garlic, tomatoes, and oregano.
3. Stuff the eggplant halves with the beef mixture.
4. Preheat the air to 360°F (180 °C). Place the stuffed eggplants in the air fryer basket and let them cook for 20 minutes or until the beef is fully cooked and the eggplants are tender.
5. Garnish with fresh parsley before serving.

Nutrition information (per serving):
Calories: 250 | Sodium: 80mg | Cholesterol: 40mg | Protein: 15g | Fat:15g | Carbohydrates 18g

Notes:

Prep. Time: 10 min   Cook Time: 12 min   Service: 4

Zesty Mahi-Mahi

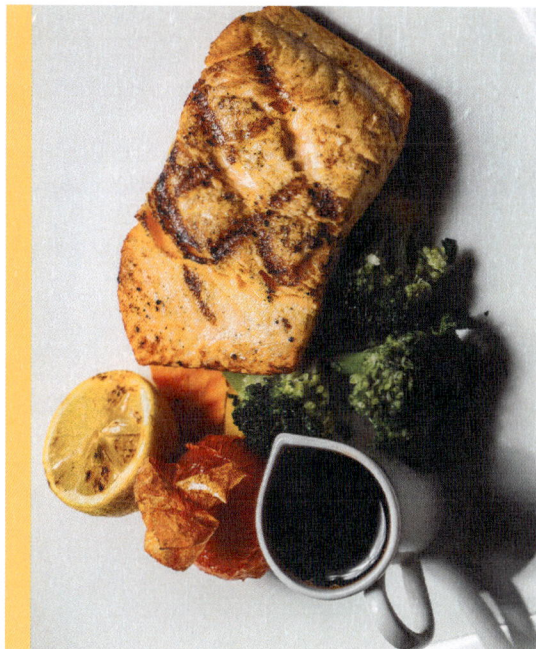

Ingredients:

- 4 Mahi-Mahi fillets (4 ounces each)
- 1 tablespoon olive oil
- 1 teaspoon garlic powder
- 1 teaspoon smoked paprika
- 1/2 teaspoon ground black pepper
- 1 lemon, halved
- 2 cups broccoli florets
- Fresh parsley, chopped for garnish

Directions:

1. Preheat your air fryer to 360°F (182°C).
2. Brush both sides of the Mahi-Mahi fillets with olive oil. Season the fillets with garlic powder, smoked paprika, and black pepper.
3. Place the seasoned fillets in the air fryer basket to cook for 10minutes, flipping halfway through.
4. Meanwhile, toss the broccoli florets with a pinch of black pepper and remaining olive oil.
5. Add the broccoli to the air fryer and cook alongside the fish for the last 2 minutes.
6. Serve the Mahi-Mahi and broccoli with a squeeze of fresh lemon juice and parsley.

Nutrition information (per serving):
Calories: 180 | Sodium: 1 0 mg | Cholesterol: 80 mg | Protein: 22 g | Fat:8 g | Carbohydrates: 6 g

Notes:

Prep. Time: 13 min   Cook Time: 10 min   Service: 4

Herbed Zucchini Sticks

Ingredients:

- 4 medium zucchini, cut into 3-inch sticks
- 1 cup panko breadcrumbs
- 1/4 cup grated Parmesan cheese
- 1 tsp garlic powder
- 1 tsp dried basil
- 1 tsp dried oregano
- 1/2 tsp black pepper
- 1/2 tsp paprika
- 2 large eggs, beaten
- Non-stick cooking spray

Directions:

1. Preheat the air fryer to 390°F (200°C).
2. Mix together the panko, Parmesan, garlic powder, basil, oregano, black pepper, and paprika.
3. Dip each zucchini stick into the beaten eggs, then dredge in the breadcrumb mixture until fully coated.
4. Arrange the zucchini sticks in a single layer in the air fryer basket. Spray it lightly with cooking spray.
5. Air fry for 1 minute, flipping halfway through until the coating is golden brown and crispy.
6. Serve hot with a side of low-sodium marinara sauce.

Nutrition information (per serving):

Calories: 180 | Sodium: 150 mg | Cholesterol: 93 mg | Protein: 9 g | Fat:7 g | Carbohydrates: 20 g

Notes:

Prep. Time: 15 min   Cook Time: 20 min   Service: 4

Spicy Mediterranean Chicken

Ingredients:

- 4 boneless, skinless chicken breasts
- 2 zucchinis, sliced into rounds
- 2 cups broccoli florets
- 2 carrots, sliced
- 2 tablespoons olive oil
- 1 teaspoon dried oregano
- 1 teaspoon dried basil
- 1/2 teaspoon garlic powder
- Black pepper to taste
- Lemon wedges for serving
- Fresh chili, thinly sliced for garnish

Directions:

1. Preheat the air fryer to 360°F (182°C).
2. Rub the chicken breasts with half of the olive oil and season with oregano, garlic powder, basil, and black pepper.
3. Next, in a separate bowl, toss the sliced zucchini, broccoli, and carrots with the remaining olive oil and the same seasoning mix.
4. Place the chicken breasts in the air fryer basket and cook for 10 minutes.
5. After 10 minutes, add the seasoned vegetables to the basket with the chicken. Cook for another 10 minutes.
6. Serve the chicken and vegetables hot, garnished with lemon wedges and fresh chili slices, and on the side for squeezing over the dish.

Nutrition information (per serving):

Calories: 250 | Sodium: 125mg | Cholesterol: 65mg | Protein: 27g | Fat:9g | Carbohydrates: 10g

Notes:

Prep. Time: 10 min   Cook Time: 20 min   Service: 4

Sweet Potato and Mushroom Medley

Ingredients:

- 2 large sweet potatoes, peeled and cubed
- 2 cups mushrooms, sliced
- 1 large onion, sliced
- 2 tablespoons olive oil
- 1 teaspoon smoked paprika
- 1/2 teaspoon garlic powder
- 1/4 teaspoon black pepper
- Fresh parsley, chopped for garnish

Directions:

1. Toss the sweet potatoes, mushrooms, and onion with olive oil, smoked paprika, garlic powder, and black pepper until everything is well coated.
2. Preheat the air fryer to 380°F (193°C). Spread the vegetable mixture in the air fryer basket in a single layer.
3. Air fry for 10 minutes, then shake or stir the vegetables and continue to air fry for another 10 minutes or until the sweet potatoes are tender.
4. Garnish the potato and mushroom medley with fresh parsley.

Nutrition information (per serving):
Calories: 200 | Sodium: 30 mg | Cholesterol: 0 mg | Protein: 3 g | Fat: 7 g | Carbohydrates: 34 g

Notes:

Prep. Time: 15 min | Cook Time: 20 min | Service: 4

Sunny Falafel

Ingredients:

- 2 cups chickpeas, soaked overnight and drained
- 1 small onion, roughly chopped
- 2 cloves garlic
- 1/2 cup fresh parsley, chopped
- 1/2 cup fresh cilantro, chopped
- 1 teaspoon cumin
- 1/2 teaspoon coriander
- 1 teaspoon baking powder
- 2 tablespoons oat flour
- Olive oil spray

Directions:

1. Place the chickpeas, onion, garlic, parsley, cilantro, cumin, and coriander in a food processor. Pulse until combined but still coarse.
2. Add baking powder and oat flour to the mixture. Pulse a few times until the mixture holds together. You may need to scrape down the sides. Form the mixture into small balls or patties about the size of a walnut.
3. Preheat the air fryer to 360°F (182°C). Spray the air fryer basket with olive oil spray to prevent sticking.
4. Place the falafel in the basket in a single layer, making sure they don't touch. Spray the falafel lightly with olive oil.
5. Air fry for 10 minutes, then turn the falafel over, spray again, and continue cooking for an additional 10 minutes or until golden brown and crispy.
6. Serve with a side of low-sodium tahini sauce and fresh lemon wedges, and garnish with parsley.

Nutrition information (per serving):

Calories: 330 | Sodium: 80 mg | Cholesterol: 0 mg | Protein: 11 g | Fat:8 g | Carbohydrates: 50 g

Notes:

Prep. Time: 15 min	Cook Time: 20 min	Service: 4

Teriyaki Turkey with Udon

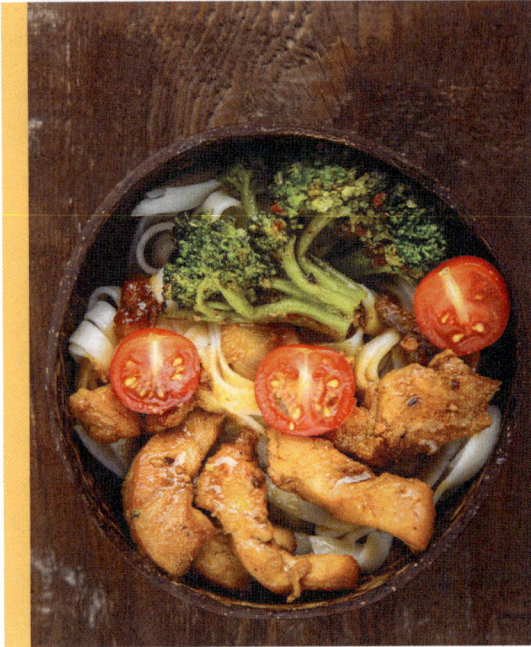

Ingredients:

- 1 pound turkey breast, sliced into strips
- 2 tablespoons low-sodium soy sauce
- 1 tablespoon honey
- 1 tablespoon rice vinegar
- 1 teaspoon grated ginger
- 2 cloves garlic, minced
- 1 teaspoon cornstarch mixed with 1 tablespoon water
- 8 ounces of udon noodles, cooked according to package instructions
- 1 head broccoli, cut into florets
- 1 cup cherry tomatoes, halved
- Non-stick Cooking spray

Directions:

1. In a bowl, whisk together the low-sodium soy sauce, honey, rice vinegar, grated ginger, and minced garlic to make the teriyaki sauce. Toss the turkey strips in the sauce and let marinate for 10 minutes.
2. Preheat the air fryer to 380°F (193°C). Place the turkey strips in the air fryer basket, making sure they are not overlapping. Cook for 0 minutes, flipping halfway through.
3. While the turkey is cooking, steam the broccoli until just tender.
4. When the turkey is done, transfer it to a pan over medium heat, pour the remaining teriyaki sauce over it, and add the cornstarch mixture. Stir until the sauce thickens.
5. Arrange the cooked udon noodles in serving bowls. Top with the air-fried turkey, steamed broccoli, and cherry tomatoes.
6. Drizzle with the thickened teriyaki sauce from the pan.

Nutrition information (per serving):
Calories: 400 | Sodium: 300mg | Cholesterol: 50mg | Protein: 30g | Fat:5g | Carbohydrates: 60g

Notes:

Prep. Time: 15 min   Cook Time: 20 min   Service: 4

Chicken Caesar Salad

Ingredients:

- 2 boneless, skinless chicken breasts
- 1 teaspoon olive oil
- 1/2 teaspoon black pepper
- 1/2 teaspoon garlic powder
- 8 cups chopped Romaine lettuce
- 1 cup cherry tomatoes, halved
- 1/4 cup shredded Parmesan cheese
- 1 cup whole-grain croutons
- Low-sodium Caesar dressing
- Lemon wedges for serving

Directions:

1. Preheat air fryer to 375°F (190°C). Rub the chicken breasts with olive oil, black pepper, and garlic powder.
2. Cook the chicken for 20 minutes. Let it rest for a few minutes, and then slice it into strips.
3. In a large bowl, mix together the chopped Romaine lettuce, cherry tomatoes, and half the amount of Parmesan cheese. Add the chicken slices to this salad mix and carefully toss everything together.
4. Top with whole grain croutons and the remaining Parmesan cheese.
5. Serve with low-sodium Caesar dressing on the side and lemon wedges.

Nutrition information (per serving):
Calories: 220 | Sodium: 180mg | Cholesterol: 65mg | Protein: 26g | Fat:7g | Carbohydrates: 12g

Notes:

Prep. Time: 10 min	Cook Time: 6 min	Service: 4

Prawn and Arugula Salad

Ingredients:

- 16 large prawns, peeled and deveined
- 4 cups arugula leaves
- 1/2 cup cherry tomatoes, halved
- 1/4 cup sliced almonds
- 1 tablespoon olive oil
- 1/2 teaspoon garlic powder
- 1/2 teaspoon black pepper
- 1 tablespoon lemon juice
- Lemon wedges for serving

Directions:

1. Toss the prawns with olive oil, garlic powder, and black pepper.
2. Preheat the air fryer to 400°F (200°C). Place the prawns in the air fryer basket and cook for 6 minutes, turning them over halfway through or until they are slightly crispy.
3. While the prawns are cooking, toast the sliced almonds in a pan without any oil over medium heat for 3-4 minutes. Keep stirring them until they turn golden and give off a nice aroma. Then take them off the stove.
4. Combine the arugula and cherry tomatoes. Drizzle with lemon juice and toss gently.
5. Let the prawns cool for a moment after cooking, then add them to the salad.
6. Top the salad with the toasted almonds, and serve with lemon wedges on the side.

Nutrition information (per serving):
Calories: 180 | Sodium: 120mg | Cholesterol: 90mg | Protein: 15g | Fat:10g | Carbohydrates: 5g

Notes:

Prep. Time: 10 min	Cook Time: 5 min	Service: 4

Seafood Delight Salad

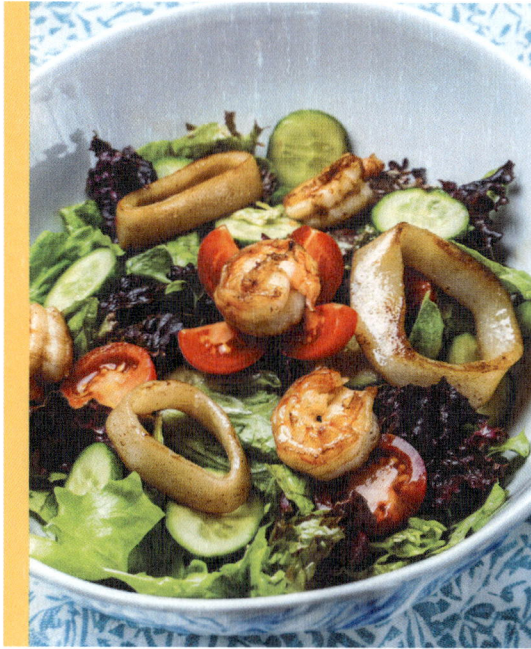

Ingredients:

- 8 large prawns, peeled and deveined
- 8 calamari rings
- 4 cups mixed salad greens (lettuce, arugula, etc.)
- 1 cup cherry tomatoes, halved
- 1/2 cucumber, thinly sliced
- 2 tablespoons olive oil
- 1/2 teaspoon garlic powder
- 1/2 teaspoon smoked paprika
- Black pepper to taste
- 1 tablespoon lemon juice
- Lemon wedges for serving

Directions:

1. In a bowl, mix 1 tablespoon of olive oil with garlic powder, smoked paprika, and black pepper. Toss the prawns and calamari in the mixture until they are well-coated.
2. Preheat the air fryer to 380°F (193°C). Place the seafood in the air fryer basket and cook for 3-5 minutes or until the prawns are pink and the calamari is tender. Let it cool for a few minutes.
3. While the seafood is cooking, arrange the mixed salad greens, cherry tomatoes, and cucumber slices in a large serving bowl.
4 Drizzle the salad with the remaining olive oil and lemon juice.
5. Serve the salad with lemon wedges on the side.

Nutrition information (per serving):
Calories: 180 | Sodium: 150mg | Cholesterol: 110mg | Protein: 15g | Fat:8g | Carbohydrates: 8g

Notes:

Prep. Time: 9 min   Cook Time: 20 min   Service: 4

Spicy Turkey Salad

Ingredients:

- 4 whole turkey breast cutlets
- 4 cups mixed salad greens
- 1 cup cherry tomatoes, halved
- 1/2 red onion, thinly sliced
- 1 tablespoon olive oil
- 1 teaspoon dried oregano
- 1 teaspoon dried basil
- 1/2 teaspoon crushed red pepper flakes
- Black pepper to taste
- 2 tablespoons balsamic vinegar
- 1 teaspoon low-sodium Dijon mustard
- 1 tablespoon sesame seeds
- 1 small fresh chili, finely sliced for garnish

Directions:

1. Preheat the air fryer to 360°F (182°C).
2. Rub the whole turkey breast cutlets with olive oil, then season with oregano, basil, crushed red pepper flakes, and black pepper.
3. Place the whole seasoned turkey breasts in the air fryer basket. Cook the turkey breasts for 20 minutes or until the outside is golden brown.
4. While the turkey is cooking, prepare the dressing by whisking together balsamic vinegar and Dijon mustard.
5. Once the turkey is cooked, allow it to rest for a few minutes. Then, slice the turkey breast cutlets into strips.
6. In a large bowl, toss the mixed salad greens with the cherry tomatoes, red onion, and fresh chili slices.
7. Drizzle the salad with the balsamic-Dijon dressing and sprinkle with sesame seeds before serving.

Nutrition information (per serving):
Calories: 220 | Sodium: 85mg | Cholesterol: 50mg | Protein: 25g | Fat:7g | Carbohydrates: 8g

Notes:

Prep. Time: 14 min   Cook Time: 11 min   Service: 4

Sesame Vegetables Salat

Ingredients:

- 1 medium zucchini, cut into matchsticks
- 2 medium carrots, peeled, cut into matchsticks
- 1 red bell pepper, deseeded, sliced thinly
- 1 tablespoon olive oil
- 1 tablespoon sesame seeds
- 1/4 teaspoon ground black pepper
- 1/4 teaspoon garlic powder

Directions:

1. Combine the carrots, zucchini, and bell pepper with olive oil, black pepper, and garlic powder.
2. Preheat the air fryer to 380°F (193°C). Put the vegetables in the air fryer basket in a single layer for even cooking.
3. Air fry for about 10 minutes, or until the vegetables are your desired tenderness, shaking the basket halfway through.
4. After air frying, sprinkle the vegetables with sesame seeds.

Nutrition information (per serving):
Calories: 80 | Sodium: 45 mg | Cholesterol: 0 mg | Protein: 2.5 g | Fat: 4.5 g | Carbohydrates: 9 g

Notes:

Prep. Time: 15 min   Cook Time: 20 min   Service: 4

Herbed Chickpea and Veggie Salad

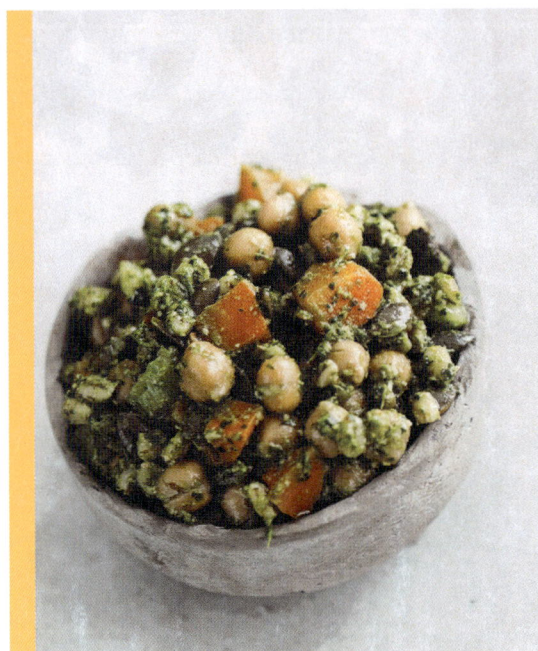

Ingredients:

- 1 can (15 ounces) chickpeas, drained and rinsed
- 1 medium zucchini, diced into small pieces
- 1 medium carrot, diced into small pieces
- 2 tablespoons olive oil
- 1 teaspoon garlic powder
- 1 teaspoon onion powder
- 2 tablespoons freshly chopped parsley
- 1 tablespoon freshly chopped basil
- 1 red bell pepper, diced into small pieces
- 1 teaspoon dried oregano
- Zest of 1 lemon
- Juice of 1/2 lemon
- Freshly ground black pepper, to taste

Directions:

1. Preheat the air fryer to 380°F (190°C).
2. In a large bowl, combine chickpeas, zucchini, carrot, and red bell pepper. Drizzle the chickpeas and vegetables with olive oil, then sprinkle garlic powder, onion powder, parsley, basil, oregano, and lemon zest over them. Toss until everything is well-coated.
3. Transfer the mixture into the air fryer basket and spread out into a single layer. Cook in the air fryer for 20 minutes, shaking the basket half way through, until the chickpeas are slightly crispy.
4. Once done, squeeze fresh lemon juice over the salad and season with black pepper to taste.

Nutrition information (per serving):

Calories: 190 kcal | Sodium: 240 mg | Cholesterol: 0 mg | Protein: 6 g | Fat: 8 g | Carbohydrates: 22 g

Notes:

Prep. Time: 12 min   Cook Time: 20 min   Service: 4

Sesame Chicken Salad

Ingredients:

- 2 boneless, skinless chicken breasts
- 1 tablespoon sesame oil
- 1 tablespoon low-sodium soy sauce
- 1 teaspoon honey
- 1 teaspoon fresh ginger, grated
- 1 garlic clove, minced
- 8 cups mixed salad greens
- 1 cup strawberries, sliced
- 2 tablespoons sesame seeds
- 1/4 cup slivered almonds
- 2 tablespoons rice vinegar
- 1 teaspoon olive oil

Directions:

1. In a small bowl, toss sesame oil, low-sodium soy sauce, honey, ginger, and garlic to create a marinade. Coat the chicken breasts with half of the marinade and let sit for 10 minutes.

2 Preheat the air fryer to 360°F (182°C). Place the chicken in the air fryer basket and cook for 20. Once cooked, slice the chicken into strips.

3. In a large bowl, toss the salad greens and sliced strawberries with rice vinegar and olive oil.

4. Divide the salad among serving plates, top with sliced chicken, sprinkle with sesame seeds, and add slivered almonds if using.

Nutrition information (per serving):

Calories: 230 | Sodium: 200mg | Cholesterol: 65mg | Protein: 27g | Fat:10g | Carbohydrates: 8g

Notes:

Prep. Time: 15 min   Cook Time: 8 min   Service: 4

Walnut & Beef Salad

Ingredients:

- 1/2 lb lean beef steak, thinly sliced
- 4 cups mixed greens
- 1 cup cherry tomatoes, halved
- 1/4 cup dried cranberries
- 1/2 cup walnuts
- 1/2 cup corn kernels, fresh or frozen
- 2 tbsp olive oil
- 1 tbsp balsamic vinegar
- 1 tsp Dijon mustard
- 1 tsp maple syrup
- Black pepper to taste

Directions:

1 In a bowl, toss the beef slices with olive oil and black pepper.
2. Preheat the air fryer to 380°F (193°C). Place the beef in the air fryer basket and then cook for about 8 minutes, flipping halfway through, until the desired doneness.
3. Combine mixed greens, cherry tomatoes, corn, and cranberries.
4. Next, whisk together 1 tablespoon olive oil, balsamic vinegar, Dijon mustard, and maple syrup to create the dressing. Toss the salad with the dressing.
5. Top the salad with air-fried beef slices and walnuts.

Nutrition information (per serving):
Calories: 320 | Sodium: 70 mg | Cholesterol: 40 mg | Protein: 24 g | Fat:20 g | Carbohydrates: 12 g

Notes:

Prep. Time: 12 min   Cook Time: 20 min   Service: 4

Spicy Teriyaki Chicken with Broccoli

Ingredients:

- 4 cups broccoli florets
- 4 boneless, skinless chicken thighs cut into bite-sized pieces
- 1 tablespoon olive oil
- 1 red chili pepper, thinly sliced
- Sesame seeds for garnish
- Spring onions, chopped for garnish
- For the low-sodium teriyaki sauce:
- 1/4 cup low-sodium soy sauce
- 1 tablespoon honey
- 1 clove garlic, minced
- 1 teaspoon grated ginger
- 1 tablespoon rice vinegar
- 1 teaspoon cornstarch mixed with 1 tablespoon water

Directions:

1. Whisk together the low-sodium soy sauce, honey, minced garlic, grated ginger, and rice vinegar. Set aside.
2. Toss the chicken pieces with half of the teriyaki sauce and olive oil.
3. Preheat the air fryer to 380°F (193°C). Place the chicken in the air fryer basket and cook for 10 minutes.
4. Meanwhile, toss the broccoli florets with the remaining olive oil.
5. After the chicken has cooked for 10 minutes, add the broccoli to the air fryer basket with the chicken. Cook for another 10 minutes.
6. While the chicken and broccoli are cooking, heat the remaining teriyaki sauce into a small saucepan over medium heat. Stir in the cornstarch and water mixture. Bring to a simmer and cook until the sauce thickens.
7. Once the chicken and broccoli are done, toss them in the thickened teriyaki sauce.
8. Serve garnished with red chili slices, sesame seeds, and spring onions.

Nutrition information (per serving):

Calories: 280 | Sodium: 350mg | Cholesterol: 80mg | Protein: 25g | Fat:12g | Carbohydrates: 15g

Notes:

Prep. Time: 14 min | Cook Time: 15 min | Service: 4

Mediterranean Eggplant and Kale Salad

Ingredients:

- 2 medium eggplants, sliced into 1/4-inch rounds
- 1 large bunch of kale, stems removed and leaves torn
- 1 red bell pepper, sliced into strips
- 1 red onion, sliced into rings
- 2 tablespoons extra virgin olive oil
- 1 teaspoon smoked paprika
- 2 tablespoons tahini
- 1 tablespoon apple cider vinegar
- 1 tablespoon lemon juice
- 1 clove garlic, minced
- 1 teaspoon ground cumin
- Freshly ground black pepper, to taste
- 1 tablespoon sesame seeds, for garnish
- Fresh parsley, chopped, for garnish

Directions:

1. Toss the eggplant slices with 1 tablespoon of olive oil and smoked paprika until evenly coated.
2. Preheat the air fryer to 375°F (190°C). Arrange the eggplant slices in the air fryer basket in a single layer and cook them for 8 minutes. After that, flip the slices over and continue to cook them for another 7 minutes, or until they're tender and have a light brown color. Set aside.
3. While the eggplant cooks, massage the kale with 1 tablespoon of olive oil in a separate bowl until the leaves start to soften.
4. Next, in a small bowl, whisk together apple cider vinegar, tahini, lemon juice, minced garlic, and cumin to make a dressing.
5. Toss the kale, red bell pepper, and red onion in the air fryer and cook for 5 minutes.
8. Arrange the cooked vegetables on a serving platter, top with the eggplant slices, drizzle with the tahini dressing, and garnish with sesame seeds and fresh parsley.

Nutrition information (per serving):
Calories: 180 kcal | Sodium: 60 mg | Cholesterol: 0 mg | Protein: 5 g | Fat:10 g | Carbohydrates: 20 g

Notes:

Prep. Time: 15 min   Cook Time: 10 min   Service: 4

Crispy Shrimp Cakes

Ingredients:

- 1 pound shrimp, peeled and deveined
- 1/4 cup almond flour
- 1 large egg
- 1/4 teaspoon garlic powder
- 1/4 teaspoon black pepper
- 1/2 teaspoon paprika
- 1/2 teaspoon dried parsley
- Olive oil spray
- 1 cup carrots, julienned for garnish
- 4 cups lettuce, shredded for garnish

Directions:

1. Finely chop the shrimp into small pieces.
2. Transfer the chopped shrimp to a bowl and mix with almond flour, egg, garlic powder, black pepper, paprika, and dried parsley. Form the mixture into small patties.
3. Preheat the air fryer to 400°F (200°C). Spray the air fryer basket with olive oil spray and place the shrimp cakes in a single layer, spraying the tops lightly as well.
4. Cook for 10 minutes, flipping halfway through, until the shrimp cakes are golden and cooked through.
5. Serve the shrimp cakes on a bed of shredded lettuce and julienned carrots.

Nutrition information (per serving):

Calories: 180 | Sodium: 200mg | Cholesterol: 220mg | Protein: 24g Fat:8g | Carbohydrates: 5g

Notes:

Prep. Time: 15 min   Cook Time: 20 min   Service: 4

Eggplant Rolls with Herbed Couscous

Ingredients:

- 2 large eggplants, sliced lengthwise into 1/4-inch thick strips
- 2 tablespoons olive oil
- 1 cup couscous
- 1 cup low-sodium vegetable broth
- 1/2 cup chopped fresh parsley
- 1/4 cup pine nuts
- 1 teaspoon turmeric
- 1 teaspoon smoked paprika
- 1/2 teaspoon black pepper
- 2 cloves garlic, minced
- 1 lemon, zested and juiced
- Fresh basil leaves for garnish
- Roasted red pepper strips for garnish

Directions:

1. Brush each eggplant slice with olive oil, then season with black pepper and smoked paprika for flavor.
2. Preheat the air fryer to 380°F (190°C). Place the eggplant slices in the basket in a single layer and cook for 8-10 minutes or until tender, turning halfway through.
3. While eggplants are cooking, bring the vegetable broth to a boil in a saucepan. Mix in the couscous, turmeric, and lemon zest, then take the saucepan off the heat. Then, cover it and let it sit for 5 minutes. Afterward, fluff the couscous with a fork and add parsley, pine nuts, minced garlic, and a splash of lemon juice.
4. Place a spoonful of couscous at one end of each eggplant slice and roll up tightly.
5. Arrange the eggplant rolls in the air fryer basket. Cook for an additional 9 minutes at 360°F (180°C).
6. Serve the eggplant rolls garnished with roasted red pepper strips and fresh basil leaves.

Nutrition information (per serving):
Calories: 300 | Sodium: 50mg | Cholesterol: 0mg | Protein: 8g | Fat: 10g | Carbohydrates: 45g

Notes:

Prep. Time: 12 min   Cook Time: 15 min   Service: 4

Vegetable Croquettes

Ingredients:

- 2 cups mashed potatoes (cooled)
- 1 cup cooked mixed vegetables (carrots, peas, corn), finely chopped
- 1/4 cup onion, finely chopped
- 2 cloves garlic, minced
- 1/2 cup almond flour
- 1/4 cup grated Parmesan cheese
- 1 teaspoon dried parsley
- Black pepper, to taste
- 1/2 cup whole wheat breadcrumbs
- Olive oil spray

Directions:

1. Combine mashed potatoes, mixed vegetables, onion, garlic, almond flour, Parmesan cheese, dried herbs, and black pepper until well combined.
2. Form the mixture into small balls, then flatten slightly to create a croquette shape.
3. Place the breadcrumbs in a shallow dish and lightly coat each croquette with breadcrumbs.
4. Preheat the air fryer to 380°F (190°C). Spray the air fryer basket with olive oil spray.
5. Place the croquettes in the basket in a single layer, ensuring they do not touch. Spray the tops with olive oil spray.
6. Cook for 15 minutes, turning halfway through or until the croquettes are golden brown and crisp.
7. Serve with a side of green salad.

Nutrition information (per serving):
Calories: 220 | Sodium: 85mg | Cholesterol: 4mg | Protein: 6g | Fat:7g | Carbohydrates: 35g

Notes:

Prep. Time: 15 min   Cook Time: 10 min   Service: 4

Herbed Cheese Balls

Ingredients:

- 2 cups low-sodium mozzarella cheese, shredded
- 1 cup almond flour
- 1 teaspoon garlic powder
- 1 teaspoon onion powder
- 1 teaspoon dried parsley
- 1/2 teaspoon black pepper
- 2 large eggs, beaten
- 1 cup panko breadcrumbs
- Non-stick cooking spray

Directions:

1. In a bowl, mix the shredded mozzarella cheese with almond flour, garlic powder, onion powder, dried parsley, and black pepper.
2. Shape the cheese mixture into small balls approximately 1 inch in diameter.
3. Dip each cheese ball into the beaten eggs, then roll them in the panko breadcrumbs until well coated.
4. Preheat the air fryer to 390°F (200°C).
5. Spray the air fryer basket with cooking spray to prevent sticking.
6. Place the cheese balls in the air fryer basket, making sure they don't touch each other. Work in batches if necessary.
7. Air fry for 10 minutes or until golden and crispy. Halfway through cooking, gently shake the basket or flip the cheese balls to ensure even cooking.
8. Serve with a side of low-sodium ketchup.

Nutrition information (per serving):
Calories: 320 | Sodium: 180 mg | Cholesterol: 110 mg | Protein: 18 g | Fat:24 g | Carbohydrates: 8 g

Notes:

Prep. Time: 25 min   Cook Time: 20 min   Service: 4

Falafel with Tahini Sauce

Ingredients:

- 2 cups chickpeas, soaked overnight and drained
- 1 small onion, roughly chopped
- 4 cloves of garlic
- 1/4 cup fresh parsley, chopped
- 1/4 cup fresh cilantro, chopped
- 1 teaspoon ground cumin
- 1 teaspoon ground coriander
- 1/4 teaspoon cayenne pepper
- 1 teaspoon baking powder
- 2 tablespoons whole wheat flour
- 2 tablespoons lemon juice
- Olive oil spray
- Freshly ground black pepper, to taste

For the Tahini Sauce:
- 1/4 cup tahini
- 2 tablespoons lemon juice
- 1 clove garlic, minced

Directions:

1. Place the chickpeas, onion, garlic, parsley, cilantro, cumin, coriander, cayenne pepper, baking powder, flour, and lemon juice in a food processor. Pulse until the mixture is coarsely ground.
2. Form the mixture into small balls, each about 1.5 inches in diameter.
3. Preheat the air fryer to 360°F (182°C). Lightly spray the falafel balls with olive oil spray and season with a salt substitute and black pepper.
4. Arrange the falafel in the air fryer basket in a single layer, ensuring they are not touching. Cook for 10 minutes, flip the falafel, then cook for another 10 minutes until golden brown and crispy.
5. For the tahini sauce, whisk together tahini, lemon juice, minced garlic, and water in a bowl until smooth.

Nutrition information (per serving):
Calories: 325 kcal | Sodium: 75 mg | Cholesterol: 0 mg | Protein: 14 g | Fat: 14 g | Carbohydrates: 42 g

Notes:

Prep. Time: 5 min   Cook Time: 12 min   Service: 4

Honey-Walnut Pears

Ingredients:

- 2 large ripe pears, halved and cored
- 2 tbsp honey
- 1/4 cup walnuts, chopped
- A pinch of ground cinnamon
- A pinch of ground nutmeg
- Fresh thyme for garnish

Directions:

1. Preheat the air fryer to 350°F (175°C).
2. Place the pear halves in the air fryer basket and cut sides up.
3. Drizzle each pear half with honey, then sprinkle with cinnamon and nutmeg. Top with chopped walnuts.
4. Air fry for 12 minutes or until the pears are soft and the walnuts are toasted.
5. Garnish with fresh thyme leaves.

Nutrition information (per serving):

Calories: 150 | Sodium: 0 mg | Cholesterol: 0 mg | Protein: 1 g | Fat: 5g | Carbohydrates: 27 g

Notes:

Prep. Time: 8 min   Cook Time: 20 min   Service: 4

Nut Stuffed Apples

Ingredients:

- 4 large Granny Smith apples
- 1/4 cup walnuts, roughly chopped
- 1/4 cup almonds, roughly chopped
- 2 tablespoons raisins
- 2 tablespoons dried cranberries
- 1/4 teaspoon ground cinnamon
- 1/8 teaspoon ground nutmeg
- 4 teaspoons maple syrup
- 1 star anise for garnish
- 4 cinnamon sticks for garnish

Directions:

1. Core the apples, making sure to create a large well in the center without puncturing the bottom.
2. In a bowl, mix together walnuts, almonds, raisins, dried cranberries, ground cinnamon, and nutmeg.
3. Fill each apple with the nut and dried fruit mixture, then top each with a teaspoon of maple syrup.
4. Preheat the air fryer to 350°F (175°C). Place the stuffed apples in the air fryer basket. Cook them for 20 minutes or until the apples are tender and the filling is warm.
5. Carefully remove the apples from the air fryer and let them cool slightly.
6. Garnish each apple with a cinnamon stick and star anise before serving.

Nutrition information (per serving):

Calories: 210 kcal | Sodium: 5 mg | Cholesterol: 0 mg | Protein: 2 g | Fat:7 g | Carbohydrates: 37 g

Notes:

Prep. Time: 12 min   Cook Time: 15 min   Service: 4

Crispy Tofu Nuggets

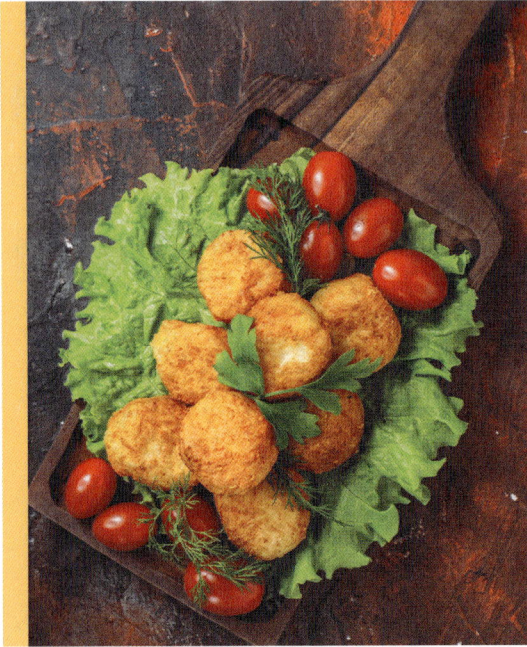

Ingredients:

- 1 block (14 oz) extra-firm tofu, pressed and cubed
- 1/2 cup unsweetened almond milk
- 1 tablespoon apple cider vinegar
- 1 cup panko breadcrumbs
- 1 teaspoon garlic powder
- 1 teaspoon onion powder
- 1 teaspoon smoked paprika
- 1/2 teaspoon ground black pepper
- Fresh parsley and dill for garnish
- Cherry tomatoes and lettuce for serving

Directions:

1. In a shallow bowl, mix almond milk and apple cider vinegar together to make a vegan "buttermilk."
2. In another shallow bowl, mix panko breadcrumbs with garlic powder, onion powder, smoked paprika, and black pepper.
3. Dip tofu cubes into the almond milk mixture, then coat with the breadcrumb mixture.
4. Preheat the air fryer to 375°F (190°C). Place the tofu nuggets in a single layer in the air fryer basket.
5. Cook for 15 minutes, flipping halfway through or until the nuggets are golden brown and crispy.
6. Serve the tofu nuggets on a bed of lettuce with cherry tomatoes and garnish with fresh parsley and dill.

Nutrition information (per serving):

Calories: 180 | Sodium: 100 mg | Cholesterol: 0 mg | Protein: 12 g | Fat:8 g | Carbohydrates: 15 g

Notes:

58

Prep. Time: 7 min   Cook Time: 20 min   Service: 4

Herbed Beetroot Fries

Ingredients:

- 4 large beetroots, peeled and cut into fries
- 1 tbsp olive oil
- 1 tsp dried thyme
- 1 tsp dried rosemary
- 1/4 tsp garlic powder
- 1/4 tsp black pepper
- Fresh dill for garnish
- Low-sodium yogurt for dipping

Directions:

1. Toss the beetroot fries with olive oil, thyme, rosemary, garlic powder, and black pepper in a bowl.
2. Preheat the air fryer to 380°F (190°C). Arrange the seasoned beetroot fries in a single layer in the air fryer basket.
3. Cook for 20 minutes, shaking the basket halfway through, until the beetroots are tender and slightly crisp on the edges.
4. Garnished with fresh dill and a side of low-sodium yogurt.

Nutrition information (per serving):
Calories: 120 | Sodium: 80 mg | Cholesterol: 0 mg | Protein: 2.5 g | Fat:3.5 g | Carbohydrates: 20 g

Notes:

Prep. Time: 15 min   Cook Time: 10 min   Service: 4

Stuffed Mushrooms with Melted Cheese

Ingredients:

- 16 large champignon mushrooms, stems removed and finely chopped (reserve the caps)
- 2 tablespoons olive oil
- 1/4 cup finely chopped walnuts
- 1/4 cup finely diced red onion
- 2 cloves garlic, minced
- 1/4 cup breadcrumbs
- 1/4 cup grated low-sodium mozzarella cheese
- 2 tablespoons fresh dill, chopped
- Freshly ground black pepper, to taste

Directions:

1. Heat 1 tablespoon of olive oil in a skillet over medium heat. Add the chopped mushroom stems, walnuts, red onion, and garlic. Sauté until the onions are translucent and the mixture is fragrant.
2. Take the skillet off the heat. Stir in breadcrumbs, half of the mozzarella cheese, and chopped dill—season with black pepper to taste.
3. Fill each mushroom cap with the stuffing mixture, then top with the remaining mozzarella cheese.
4. Preheat the air fryer to 360°F (182°C). Brush the outside of the mushroom caps with the remaining olive oil and arrange them in the air fryer basket.
5. Air fry for 8-10 minutes or until the mushrooms are tender and the cheese has melted.
6. Garnish with additional fresh dill before serving.

Nutrition information (per serving):
Calories: 150 kcal | Sodium: 70 mg | Cholesterol: 5 mg | Protein: 6 g | Fat:11 g | Carbohydrates: 8 g

Notes:

Fish and Seafood

Prep. Time: 13 min   Cook Time: 10 min   Service: 4

Crispy Coconut Shrimp

Ingredients:

- 16 large shrimp, peeled and deveined, tails on
- 1/2 cup shredded unsweetened coconut
- 1/2 cup panko breadcrumbs
- 1/4 cup cornstarch
- 1 large egg
- 1/2 teaspoon garlic powder
- 1/2 teaspoon paprika
- Freshly ground black pepper, to taste
- Olive oil spray

Directions:

1. Dry the shrimp thoroughly with paper towels. Then, season them with garlic powder, paprika, and black pepper.
2. Spread cornstarch in one shallow dish. Beat an egg in a second dish. In a third dish, combine shredded coconut with panko breadcrumbs.
3. Coat each shrimp in cornstarch first, tapping off the extra, then dip them in the egg, and lastly, roll them in the coconut-panko mix.
4. Heat your air fryer to 400°F (200°C). Place the shrimp in the air fryer basket in one layer, ensuring they don't overlap. Mist them lightly with olive oil spray.
5. Cook the shrimp for 10 minutes, turning them over once halfway, until they turn golden brown and are fully cooked.

Nutrition information (per serving):
Calories: 250 | Sodium: 150mg | Cholesterol: 115mg | Protein: 12g | Fat:12g | Carbohydrates: 20g

Notes:

Prep. Time: 10 min   Cook Time: 12 min   Service: 4

Golden Fish Fillets

Ingredients:

- 4 cod fillets
- 1/2 cup almond flour
- 1 teaspoon garlic powder
- 1/2 teaspoon paprika
- 1/2 teaspoon black pepper
- Olive oil spray
- Cherry tomatoes for garnish

Directions:

1. Combine almond flour, garlic powder, paprika, and black pepper in a bowl.
2. Dry the fillets with paper towels. Coat each fish fillet evenly with the almond flour mixture on both sides.
3. Preheat the air fryer to 390°F (200°C).
4. Spray the air fryer basket with olive oil spray and place the fish fillets in the basket.
5. Cook the fish for 12 minutes or until the coating turns golden and crispy.
6. Garnished the fish fillets with fresh cherry tomatoes on the side.

Nutrition information (per serving):
Calories: 220 | Sodium: 80mg | Cholesterol: 80mg | Protein: 23g | Fat:10g | Carbohydrates: 3g

Notes:

Prep. Time: 10 min   Cook Time: 15 min   Service: 4

Salmon Steak with Vegetable Rice

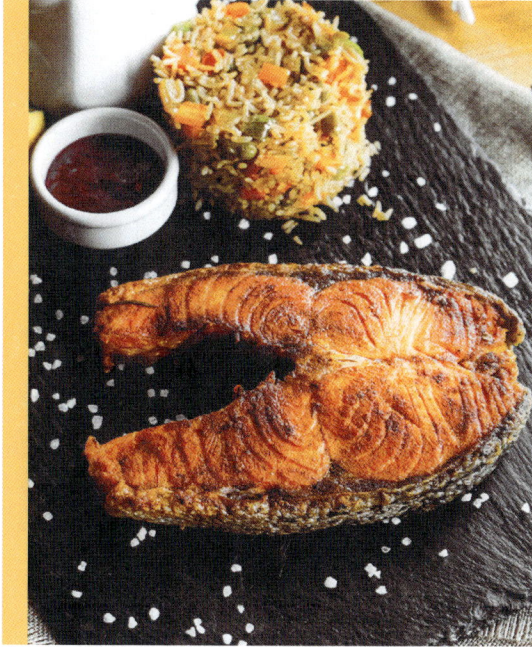

Ingredients:

- 4 salmon steaks
- 1 tablespoon olive oil
- 1 lemon, zested and juiced
- 1 teaspoon garlic powder
- 1 teaspoon onion powder
- 1 teaspoon dried dill
- 1 teaspoon paprika
- Black pepper, to taste
- 2 cups cooked brown rice
- 1 cup mixed vegetables (carrots, peas, and corn)
- 1 tablespoon fresh parsley, chopped
- 1 tablespoon fresh cilantro, chopped
- 1/4 cup pomegranate seeds, for garnish
- Lemon slices, for garnish

Directions:

1. Mix olive oil, lemon zest, lemon juice, garlic powder, onion powder, dill, paprika, and black pepper. Brush the mixture over both sides of the fish steaks.
2. Preheat the air fryer to 400°F (200°C). Place the fish steaks in the basket, skin side down, and cook for 10-13 minutes, or until the fish easily flakes apart when tested with a fork.
3. Next, in a skillet over medium heat, sauté the mixed vegetables until tender, about 5 minutes. Stir in the cooked rice, parsley, and cilantro. Cook for an additional 2 minutes.
4. Serve the fish steaks with a side of herbed vegetable rice. Garnish with pomegranate seeds and lemon slices.

Nutrition information (per serving):
Calories: 350 | Sodium: 70mg | Cholesterol: 55mg | Protein: 25g | Fat:10g | Carbohydrates: 35g

Notes:

Prep. Time: 10 min | Cook Time: 8 min | Service: 4

Smoky Mackerel Salad

Ingredients:

- 4 mackerel fillets
- 1 teaspoon olive oil
- 1 teaspoon smoked paprika
- 1/2 teaspoon garlic powder
- 1/2 teaspoon ground black pepper
- 4 cups mixed salad greens
- 1 cup cherry tomatoes, halved
- 1/4 red onion, thinly sliced
- 1 lemon, cut into wedges
- A handful of fresh parsley, chopped

Directions:

1. Rub the mackerel fillets with olive oil, smoked paprika, garlic powder, and black pepper.
2. Preheat the air fryer to 360°F (182°C). Place the mackerel fillets in the air fryer basket and then cook for 7-8 minutes, or until the fish is cooked through and the skin is slightly crispy. Let it rest for a minute.
3. While the fish is cooking, assemble the salad by tossing the mixed greens, cherry tomatoes, and red onion in a large bowl.
4. Garnish the salad with lemon wedges and chopped parsley.

Nutrition information (per serving):
Calories: 230 | Sodium: 90mg | Cholesterol: 75mg | Protein: 24g | Fat:13g | Carbohydrates: 4g

Notes:

Prep. Time: 12 min   Cook Time: 10 min   Service: 4

Sesame-Crusted Tilapia

Ingredients:

- 4 tilapia fillets
- 1/2 cup panko breadcrumbs
- 1 tablespoon sesame seeds
- 1/2 teaspoon garlic powder
- 1/4 teaspoon ground black pepper
- 2 large eggs
- Non-stick cooking spray

Directions:

1. Mix panko breadcrumbs, sesame seeds, garlic powder, and black pepper in a small bowl. In a separate bowl, beat the eggs.
2. First, dip each tilapia fillet into the egg, then coat thoroughly with the breadcrumb mixture, making sure to press the breadcrumbs onto the fillet for a good coat.
3. Preheat the air fryer to 375°F (190°C). Spray the air fryer basket with cooking spray and place the breaded fillets in the basket in a single layer, making sure they do not touch.
4. Cook the tilapia fillets for 10 minutes or until the fish easily flakes apart when tested with a fork.
5. Garnished the fish with additional sesame seeds.

Nutrition information (per serving):

Calories: 220 | Sodium: 125 mg | Cholesterol: 100 mg | Protein: 23 g | Fat:6 g | Carbohydrates: 12 g

Notes:

Prep. Time: 15 min   Cook Time: 20 min   Service: 4

Cod Cutlets with Roasted Vegetables

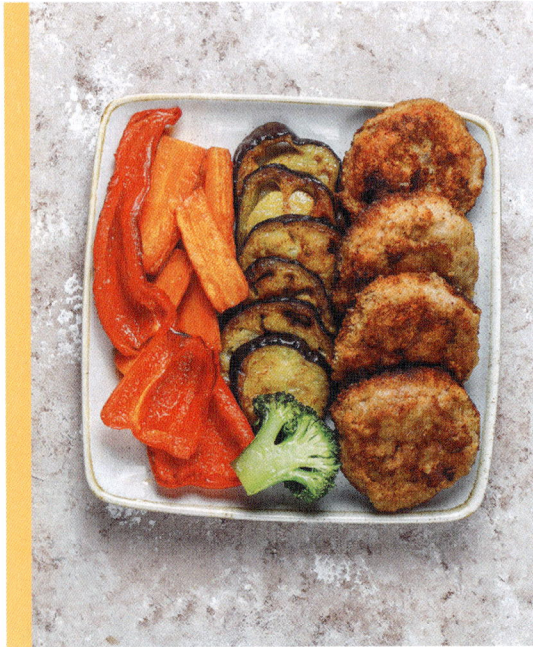

Ingredients:

- 4 cod fillets, minced
- 1/2 cup almond flour
- 1 large egg, beaten
- 1/2 cup additional almond flour for coating
- 1 teaspoon garlic powder
- 1 teaspoon onion powder
- Black pepper to taste
- Olive oil spray
- 2 medium zucchinis, sliced into rounds
- 2 red bell peppers, sliced
- 2 large carrots, peeled, cut into sticks
- 1 head of broccoli, cut into florets

Directions:

1. Mix together the minced cod, 1/2 cup almond flour, garlic powder, onion powder, and black pepper. Form the mixture into patties.
2. Set up a breading station with two plates: one with beaten egg and one with the additional almond flour for coating. Dip each fish patty into the beaten egg, then coat it with almond flour.
3. Preheat the air fryer to 380°F (193°C). Spray the air fryer basket with olive oil spray. Place the breaded cod cutlets in the basket and spray the tops with olive oil.
4. Air fry for 10 minutes, then gently flip the cutlets and cook for another 10 minutes or until the fish easily flakes apart when tested with a fork.
5. For the vegetables, spray them lightly with olive oil spray and season with black pepper. Place them in the air fryer with the fish cutlets during the last 10 minutes of cooking, or cook them in batches if necessary.
6. Serve the air-fried cod cutlets alongside the roasted vegetables.

Nutrition information (per serving):

Calories: 320 | Sodium: 100mg | Cholesterol: 80mg | Protein: 28g | Fat:12g | Carbohydrates: 18g

Notes:

Prep. Time: 10 min   Cook Time: 6 min   Service: 4

Sesame-Seared Tuna

Ingredients:

- 4 tuna steaks (about 6 ounces each)
- 2 tablespoons sesame oil
- 1 tablespoon freshly ground black pepper
- 2 tablespoons white sesame seeds
- 2 tablespoons black sesame seeds
- Fresh cilantro leaves for garnish
- Sliced green onions for garnish
- Low sodium soy sauce for dipping

Directions:

1. Brush each tuna steak with sesame oil and coat with freshly ground black pepper.
2. Mix white and black sesame seeds on a plate and press each side of the tuna steaks into the sesame seeds to ensure an even coating.
3. Preheat the air fryer to 390°F (200°C). Arrange the tuna steaks in the air fryer basket without them overlapping.
4. Cook for 3 minutes on one side, then flip the steaks and cook for an additional 3 minutes on the other side for medium-rare or longer for desired doneness.
6. Garnish with fresh thymine.

Nutrition information (per serving):
Calories: 240 | Sodium: 50 mg | Cholesterol: 60 mg | Protein: 40 g | Fat:10 g | Carbohydrates: 1 g

Notes:

Prep. Time: 12 min   Cook Time: 18 min   Service: 4

Herb-Crusted Fish

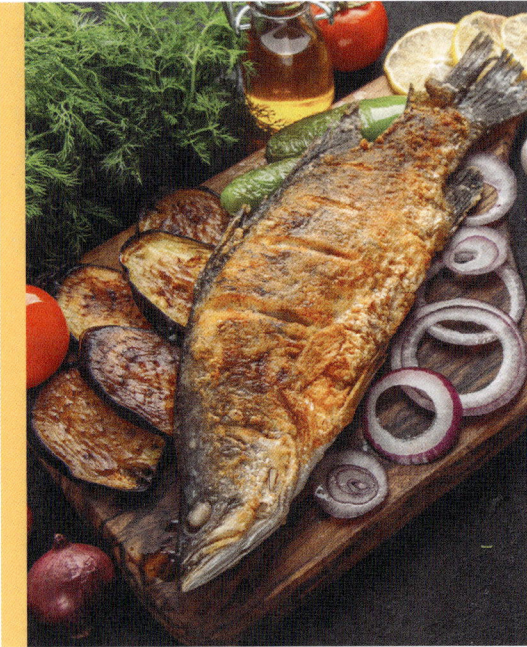

Ingredients:

- 1 whole rainbow trout, gutted and scaled
- 2 tablespoons olive oil
- 1 teaspoon freshly ground black pepper
- 1 tablespoon dried mixed herbs (thyme, rosemary, and oregano)
- 2 garlic cloves, minced
- 1 lemon, sliced into rounds
- Fresh dill for garnish
- Roasted eggplant and onion for serving

Directions:

1. Rinse the fish inside and out, and pat dry with paper towels.
2. Rub the fish with olive oil, then season both the inside and outside with pepper and mixed herbs (leave 1 tablespoon of herbs for eggplant). Place minced garlic inside the cavity. Arrange lemon slices inside the fish cavity.
3. Preheat the air fryer to 360°F (182°C). Place the fish in the air fryer basket. Cook for 15-18 minutes, or until the fish is cooked through and flakes easily with a fork. Set aside.
4. Slice the eggplant into 1-inch thick rounds. Toss the eggplant slices with the leftover. Place the herbed eggplant slices in the air fryer and cook at 390°F (200°C) for 10 minutes, flipping halfway through, until they are tender and slightly golden.
7. Garnish the fish with fresh dill and grilled eggplant before serving.

Nutrition information (per serving):
Calories: 200 | Sodium: 70 mg | Cholesterol: 60 mg | Protein: 23 g | Fat:10 g | Carbohydrates: 1 g

Notes:

Prep. Time: 15 min   Cook Time: 8 min   Service: 4

Herb-Grilled Lobster Tails

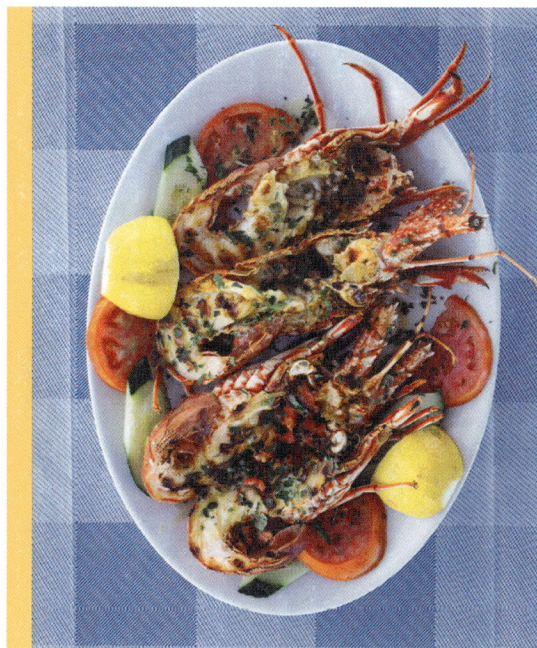

Ingredients:

- 4 lobster tails, split and cleaned
- 2 tablespoons olive oil
- 1 clove garlic, minced
- 1 teaspoon fresh thyme, chopped
- 1 teaspoon fresh rosemary, chopped
- 1 teaspoon fresh parsley, chopped
- 1/4 teaspoon black pepper
- 1 lemon, zested and juiced
- Fresh herbs and lemon wedges for garnish

Directions:

1. In a bowl, mix garlic, thyme, olive oil, rosemary, parsley, black pepper, and half of the lemon juice.
3. Brush the mixture over the lobster tails, ensuring it gets into the flesh.
4. Preheat the Air Fryer to 380°F (193°C). Arrange the lobster tails in the air fryer basket with the shell side facing down.
5. Cook for 7-8 minutes or until the meat is opaque and slightly browned.
6. Garnish with lemon zest, remaining lemon juice, and fresh herbs before serving.

Nutrition information (per serving):
Calories: 200 | Sodium: 120 mg | Cholesterol: 60 mg | Protein: 23 g | Fat:8 g | Carbohydrates: 2 g

Notes:

Prep. Time: 17 min   Cook Time: 6 min   Service: 4

Zesty Grilled Shrimp Skewers

Ingredients:

- 24 large shrimp, peeled and deveined
- 2 tablespoons olive oil
- 2 cloves garlic, minced
- 1 teaspoon smoked paprika
- 1 teaspoon dried oregano
- 1/4 teaspoon black pepper
- Juice of 1 lemon
- 1 tablespoon fresh parsley, finely chopped
- Wooden skewers, soaked

Directions:

1. Mix olive oil, garlic, smoked paprika, black pepper, oregano, and lemon juice in a bowl to make a marinade. Add the shrimp to this mixture and refrigerate for 15 minutes to marinate. 2. After marinating, thread the shrimp onto the soaked skewers.
4. Preheat the Air Fryer to 400°F (200°C).
5. Place the shrimp skewers in the Air Fryer basket and cook for 6minutes, turning halfway through, until the shrimp turn pink and are fully cooked.
6. Garnish with fresh parsley before serving.

Nutrition information (per serving):

Calories: 960 | Sodium: 150 mg | Cholesterol: 965 mg | Protein: 148 g | Fat:53 g | Carbohydrates: 61g

Notes:

Prep. Time: 12 min   Cook Time: 25 min   Service: 4

Herb-Crusted Chicken

Ingredients:

- 4 boneless, skinless chicken breasts
- 2 tablespoons olive oil
- 1 teaspoon garlic powder
- 1 teaspoon onion powder
- 1 teaspoon dried thyme
- 1 teaspoon dried rosemary
- 1 teaspoon dried parsley
- ½ teaspoon ground black pepper
- Fresh rosemary sprigs for garnish
- Fresh pomegranate seeds for garnish

Directions:

1. In a small bowl, combine dried thyme, rosemary, parsley, onion powder, garlic powder, and black pepper to make the herb seasoning.
2. Brush each chicken breast with olive oil and then rub the herb seasoning over all sides of the chicken.
3. Preheat your air fryer to 360°F (182 °C) and place the chicken breasts in the air fryer basket without overlapping them. Cook for 22-25minutes, turning halfway through the cooking time.
4. After cooking, let the chicken rest for 5 minutes before slicing.
5. Serve garnished with fresh rosemary sprigs and pomegranate seeds.

Nutrition information (per serving):
Calories: 200 | Sodium: 70 mg | Cholesterol: 65mg | Protein: 26 g | Fat:7g | Carbohydrates: 20g

Notes:

Prep. Time: 10 min   Cook Time: 20 min   Service: 4

Pork Steak with Roasted Tomatoes

Ingredients:

- 4 pork steaks
- 2 tablespoons olive oil
- 1 tablespoon fresh rosemary, finely chopped
- Black pepper to taste
- 1 red onion, cut into wedges
- 2 cups cherry tomatoes, halved
- Fresh rosemary sprigs forgarnish

Directions:

1. Brush the pork steaks with olive oil and season with chopped rosemary and black pepper.
2. Preheat the air fryer to 380°F (193°C). Place the steaks in the air fryer basket and cook for 10 minutes.
3. Flip the pork steaks and add the onion wedges and cherry tomatoes to the basket. Cook for an additional 10-15 minutes. Let the pork steaks rest for3 minutes.
4. Plate the pork steaks and top with the roasted onions and tomatoes. Garnish with fresh rosemary sprigs.

Nutrition information (per serving):

Calories: 350 | Sodium: 80mg | Cholesterol: 90mg | Protein: 25g | Fat:20g | Carbohydrates: 8g

Notes:

Prep. Time: 10 min   Cook Time: 20 min   Service: 4

Turkey Spiral Sausage

Ingredients:

- 4 low-sodium turkey spiral sausages
- 2 zucchinis, sliced into rounds
- 1 bell pepper, deseeded and sliced
- 2 tablespoons olive oil
- 1 teaspoon garlic powder
- 1 teaspoon onion powder
- 1 teaspoon dried parsley
- 1 teaspoon dried basil
- Black pepper to taste
- Fresh basil for garnish

Directions:

1. In a bowl, toss the sliced zucchini and bell pepper with olive oil, garlic powder, onion powder, dried parsley, dried basil, and black pepper.
2. Preheat your air fryer to 360°F (182°C). Place the spiral sausage in the center of the air fryer basket. Arrange the seasoned vegetables around the sausage.
3. Air fry for 20 minutes, flipping the vegetables halfway through.
4. Garnish with fresh basil leaves.

Nutrition information (per serving):
Calories: 280 | Sodium: 450mg | Cholesterol: 60mg | Protein: 22g | Fat: 18g | Carbohydrates: 5g

Notes:

Prep. Time: 15 min   Cook Time: 25 min   Service: 4

Honey Garlic Chicken Wings

Ingredients:

- 2 pounds chicken wings, tips removed and split at the joint
- 1 tablespoon olive oil
- 1 teaspoon garlic powder
- 1 teaspoon onion powder
- 1 teaspoon smoked paprika
- 1/4 cup low-sodium soy sauce
- 3 tablespoons honey
- 1 tablespoon apple cider vinegar
- 2 cloves garlic, minced
- Freshly ground black pepper, to taste
- Sesame seeds, for garnish
- Fresh basil leaves for garnish

Directions:

1. Toss the chicken wings with olive oil, garlic powder, onion powder, smoked paprika, and black pepper until evenly coated.
2. Preheat the air fryer to 380°F (193°C). Lay the wings out in the air fryer basket in one layer and cook for 20-25 minutes, turning them over half way through, until crispy.
3. For the sauce, whisk together the low-sodium apple cider vinegar, honey, soy sauce, and minced garlic in a bowl.
4. Once the wings are done, place them in a large bowl and then pour the honey garlic sauce over them. Toss to coat evenly.
5. Serve the wings garnished with sesame seeds and fresh basil leaves.

Nutrition information (per serving):
Calories: 350 | Sodium: 280mg | Cholesterol: 85mg | Protein: 22g | Fat:22g | Carbohydrates: 14g

Notes:

Prep. Time: 10 min   Cook Time: 20 min   Service: 4

Turkey Breast with Broccoli

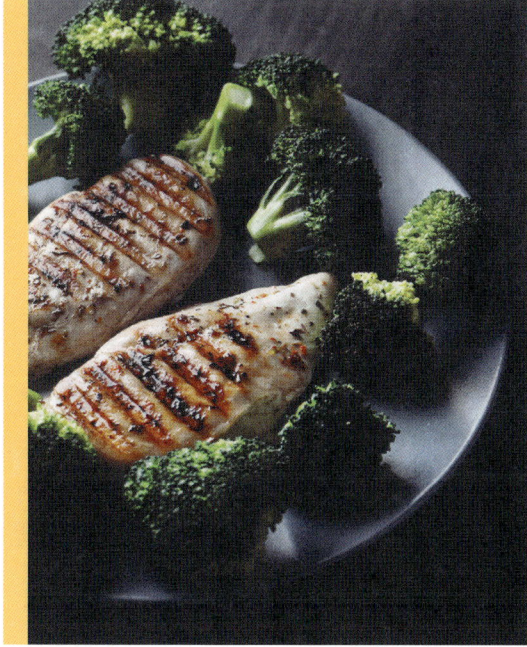

Ingredients:

- 2 turkey breast fillets, approximately 1 lb
- 1 tablespoon olive oil
- 1 teaspoon dried oregano
- 1 teaspoon dried basil
- 1/2 teaspoon garlic powder
- 1/2 teaspoon onion powder
- 1/4 teaspoon cracked black pepper
- 4 cups fresh broccoli florets

Directions:

1. Pat the turkey breast fillets dry with paper towels.
2. In a small bowl, mix the oregano, garlic powder, basil, onion powder, black pepper and olive oil.
3. Brush the herb mixture over the turkey fillets, ensuring both sides are well-coated.
4. Preheat the air fryer to 360°F (182°C). Place the turkey breasts in the air fryer basket and cook for 10 minutes.
5. Add the broccoli florets to the basket with the turkey and cook for an additional 10 minutes.
6. Remove the turkey and broccoli from the air fryer, let the turkey rest for a few minutes, then slice before serving.

Nutrition information (per serving):
Calories: 220 | Sodium: 70mg | Cholesterol: 55mg | Protein: 28g | Fat:10g | Carbohydrates: 5g

Notes:

Prep. Time: 15 min   Cook Time: 10 min   Service: 4

Smokey Beef and Cherry Tomato

Ingredients:

- 1 lb beef sirloin, cut into 1-inch cubes
- 16 cherry tomatoes
- 1 large red onion, cut into chunks
- 2 tablespoons olive oil
- 1 teaspoon smoked paprika
- 1 teaspoon garlic powder
- 1 teaspoon onion powder
- 1/2 teaspoon ground black pepper
- 1/2 teaspoon dried oregano
- 4 wooden skewers, soaked

Directions:

1. In a bowl, combine the beef cubes with olive oil, smoked paprika, garlic powder, onion powder, black pepper, and dried oregano. Mix well to ensure all pieces are evenly coated with the seasoning.
2. Thread the beef, cherry tomatoes, and red onion chunks alternately onto the soaked skewers.
3. Preheat the air fryer to 400°F (200°C). Place the skewers in the air fryer basket, making sure they don't touch each other for even cooking.
4. Cook for 10 minutes, flipping the beef halfway through or until it reaches your preferred level of doneness.
5. Serve the skewers hot with a side of low-sodium dipping sauce if desired.

Nutrition information (per serving):

Calories: 280 kcal | Sodium: 70 mg | Cholesterol: 70 mg | Protein: 26 g| Fat: 18 g | Carbohydrates: 5 g

Notes:

Prep. Time: 15 min   Cook Time: 35 min   Service: 4

Honey-Soy Glazed Beef Ribs

Ingredients:

- 4 large beef ribs
- 2 tablespoons honey
- 1/4 cup low-sodium soy sauce
- 1 tablespoon apple cider vinegar
- 2 cloves garlic, minced
- 1 teaspoon fresh ginger, grated
- 1/2 teaspoon black pepper
- 1/2 teaspoon smoked paprika
- Olive oil spray

For the pickled vegetables:
- 1/2 cup white vinegar
- 1/2 cup water
- 1 tablespoon honey
- 1 teaspoon salt substitute
- 1/2 cup sliced carrots
- 1/2 cup sliced cucumbers
- 1/2 cup sliced onions

Directions:

1. In a bowl, whisk the honey, low-sodium soy sauce, apple cider vinegar, garlic, ginger, black pepper, and smoked paprika to create the marinade.

2. Coat the beef ribs with the marinade and let them sit in the refrigerator for at least 1 hour.

3. Preheat the air fryer to 380°F (193°C). Place the marinated ribs in the air fryer basket. Cook for 35 minutes or until the meat is cooked to your liking. Spray lightly with olive oil midway through cooking.

4. For the pickled vegetables, bring the white vinegar, water, honey, and salt substitute to a boil. Pour the hot mixture over the sliced carrots, cucumbers, and onions. Refrigerate it until ready to serve.

5. Serve the ribs hot with a side of chilled pickled vegetables.

Nutrition information (per serving):
Calories: 600 kcal | Sodium: 200 mg | Cholesterol: 120 mg | Protein: 40g | Fat: 35 g | Carbohydrates: 15 g

Notes:

Prep. Time: 12 min   Cook Time: 12 min   Service: 4

Herb and Spice Pork Kebabs

Ingredients:

- 500 g pork tenderloin, cut into 1-inch cubes
- 1 tbsp olive oil
- 1 tsp smoked paprika
- 1/2 tsp dried oregano
- 1/2 tsp dried thyme
- 1/4 tsp black pepper
- 1/4 tsp onion powder
- Wooden skewers, soaked

Directions:

1. In a bowl, combine olive oil, smoked paprika, onion powder, oregano, thyme, and black pepper to create a rub.
2. Toss the pork cubes in the rub until they are well-coated. Let the meat marinate for at least 20 minutes to absorb the flavors. Thread the marinated pork onto the skewers, spacing the pieces evenly.
3. Preheat the air fryer to 390°F (200°C). Put the skewers in the air fryer basket, making sure they do not overlap for consistent cooking.
4. Cook for 12 minutes, turning the skewers halfway through or until the pork is cooked thoroughly and has a slight char on the edges.
5. Allow the skewers to rest for a couple of minutes before serving.

Nutrition information (per serving):
Calories: 210 | Sodium: 65mg | Cholesterol: 75mg | Protein: 23g | Fat:11g | Carbohydrates: 1g

Notes:

Prep. Time: 12 min   Cook Time: 20 min   Service: 4

Rustic Chicken Goulash

Ingredients:

- 1 lb chicken breast, cut into cubes
- 2 red bell peppers, sliced
- 1 large onion, chopped
- 3 cloves garlic, minced
- 1 can (14 oz) no-salt-added diced tomatoes
- 1 tablespoon Hungarian paprika
- 1 teaspoon dried marjoram
- 1 teaspoon caraway seeds
- 1/2 teaspoon black pepper
- 1 tablespoon olive oil
- Fresh parsley, chopped, for garnish

Directions:

1. In a large bowl, toss chicken cubes, onions, bell peppers, garlic, olive oil, paprika, marjoram, caraway seeds, and black pepper.
2. Preheat the air fryer to 360°F (182°C). Place the chicken and vegetable mixture in the air fryer basket. Cook them for 10 minutes, shaking the basket halfway through.
3. Add the diced tomatoes to the basket, mixing them with the chicken and vegetables. Continue cooking for 10 minutes more or until the chicken is fully cooked.
4. Garnish with fresh parsley before serving.

Nutrition information (per serving):

Calories: 250 kcal | Sodium: 75 mg | Cholesterol: 65 mg | Protein: 27 g| Fat: 7 g | Carbohydrates: 15 g

Notes:

Prep. Time: 15 min   Cook Time: 15 min   Service: 4

Crispy Turkey Cutlets with Feta Crust

Ingredients:

- 1 pound minced chicken
- 1 cup all-purpose flour
- 2 large eggs, beaten
- 1 cup crumbled feta cheese
- 1 teaspoon garlic powder
- 1 teaspoon onion powder
- 1 teaspoon paprika
- 1/2 teaspoon ground black pepper
- Olive oil spray

Directions:

1. Combine minced chicken, garlic powder, crumbled feta cheese, paprika, and onion powder in a bowl until thoroughly mixed. Shape the mixture into patties.
2. Place beaten eggs in one bowl and flour in another bowl. Dip each patty first into the egg, ensuring it's fully coated, then roll it in the flour.
3. Preheat the air fryer to 375°F (190°C) and lightly coat the air fryer basket with olive oil. Arrange the patties in the basket, spaced apart so they don't touch.
4. Air fry for 15 minutes or until the patties are golden brown and cooked through, flipping them halfway through the cooking time.
5. Allow the patties to rest for 3 minutes before serving.

Nutrition information (per serving):
Calories: 370 kcal | Sodium: 200 mg | Cholesterol: 155 mg | Protein: 35g | Fat: 12 g | Carbohydrates: 22 g

Notes:

Prep. Time: 12 min   Cook Time: 25 min   Service: 4

Rustic Potatoes and Chanterelles

Ingredients:

- 1.5 pounds of baby potatoes, halved
- 2 cups cremini mushrooms, cleaned and quartered
- 2 tablespoons olive oil
- 2 cloves garlic, minced
- 1 tablespoon fresh thyme leaves
- 1/2 teaspoon red pepper flakes
- 1/4 teaspoon smoked paprika
- Freshly ground black pepper, to taste
- 2 tablespoons green onions, sliced for garnish

Directions:

1. In a large bowl, toss the baby potatoes with 1 tablespoon of olive oil, minced garlic, thyme, red pepper flakes, smoked paprika, and black pepper until the potatoes are evenly coated with the spice mixture.

2. Preheat your air fryer to 380°F (193°C). Arrange the seasoned potatoes in the air fryer basket in a single. Air fry the potatoes for 15minutes, giving the basket a shake halfway through to ensure they brown evenly.

3. While the potatoes cook, toss the cremini mushrooms with the remaining olive oil.

4. After 15 minutes, add the mushrooms to the basket with the potatoes and air fry for an additional 10 minutes, or until the potatoes are crispy and golden and the mushrooms are tender.

5. Garnish the vegetables with sliced green onions.

Nutrition information (per serving):

Calories: 220 | Sodium: 30mg | Cholesterol: 0mg | Protein: 5g | Fat: 7g | Carbohydrates: 35g

Notes:

Prep. Time: 10 min   Cook Time: 15 min   Service: 4

Herbed Vegetable Medley

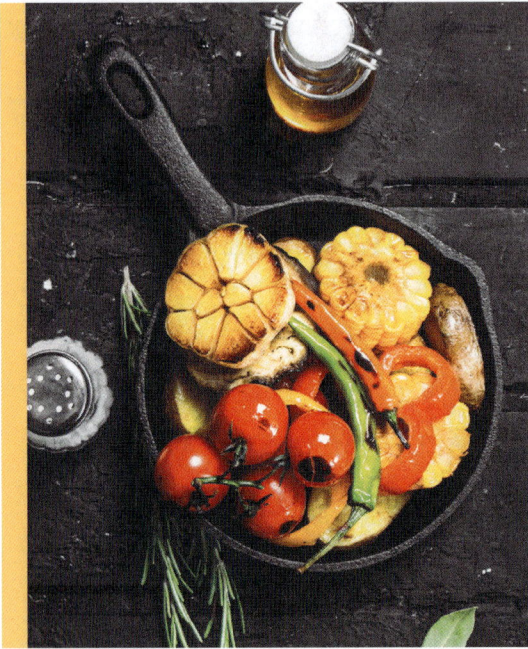

Ingredients:

- 1 garlic bulb, top sliced off to expose cloves
- 2 medium yellow corn cobs, cut into rounds
- 2 large tomatoes, quartered
- 1 red bell pepper, seeded, and cut into strips
- 1 green bell pepper, seeded and cut into strips
- 1 zucchini, sliced into rounds
- 1 tablespoon olive oil
- 1 teaspoon fresh rosemary, chopped
- 1 teaspoon fresh thyme, leaves stripped
- Freshly ground black pepper, to taste
- Sprigs of fresh rosemary for garnish

Directions:

1. In a large bowl, toss the garlic bulb, corn rounds, tomato quarters, bell pepper strips, and zucchini slices with olive oil, chopped rosemary, and thyme leaves. Season with black pepper.
2. Preheat the air fryer to 380°F (193°C). Place the vegetables in the air fryer basket in a single layer. Cook for 15 minutes, shaking half way through, or until tender.
3. Garnish the vegetables with additional fresh rosemary sprigs.

Nutrition information (per serving):
Calories: 120 | Sodium: 20mg | Cholesterol: 0mg | Protein: 3g | Fat: 4g| Carbohydrates: 20g

Notes:

Prep. Time: 10 min   Cook Time: 20 min   Service: 4

Sweet Potato Chunks

Ingredients:

- 4 medium sweet potatoes, peeled and cut into 1-inch cubes
- 2 tablespoons olive oil
- 1 teaspoon dried rosemary
- 1 teaspoon dried thyme
- 1/2 teaspoon garlic powder
- 1/2 teaspoon onion powder
- Fresh rosemary sprig for garnish

Directions:

1. In a large bowl, mix sweet potato cubes with onion powder, garlic powder, olive oil, dried rosemary, and dried thyme until evenly coated.
2. Preheat the air fryer to 380°F (193°C). Arrange the sweet potato cubes in the air fryer basket in a single layer. Air fry for 10 minutes, then shake the basket or turn the cubes with tongs.
3. Continue to air fry for another 10 minutes or until the sweet potatoes are tender and the edges are crispy.
4. Serve hot, garnished with a sprig of fresh rosemary.

Nutrition information (per serving):
Calories: 200 | Sodium: 20 mg | Cholesterol: 0 mg | Protein: 2 g | Fat: 7 g | Carbohydrates: 35 g

Notes:

Prep. Time: 10 min   Cook Time: 20 min   Service: 4

Lemon-Herb Cauliflower Steaks

Ingredients:

- 1 large head of cauliflower, sliced into 1/2 inch steaks
- 2 tablespoons olive oil
- Zest of 1 lemon
- 2 tablespoons lemon juice
- 1 teaspoon dried oregano
- 1 teaspoon dried thyme
- 1/2 teaspoon garlic powder
- 1/4 teaspoon ground black pepper
- 2 tablespoons chopped fresh parsley
- 1 tablespoon capers
- Red pepper flakes for garnish

Directions:

1. In a small bowl, whisk together olive oil, lemon zest, lemon juice, oregano, thyme, garlic powder, and black pepper to create a marinade. Brush each cauliflower steak with the marinade on both sides.
2. Preheat the air fryer to 380°F (193°C). Place the marinated cauliflower steaks in the air fryer basket in a single layer.
3. Air fry them for 10 minutes, then flip the steaks and continue cooking for another 10 minutes or until tender and the edges are golden brown.
4. Garnish with fresh parsley and capers. For a spicy kick, add red pepper flakes.

Nutrition information (per serving):
Calories: 120 kcal | Sodium: 70 mg | Cholesterol: 0 mg | Protein: 4 g | Fat:7 g | Carbohydrates: 12 g

Notes:

84

Prep. Time: 9 min   Cook Time: 8 min   Service: 4

Air Fryer Zucchini Rounds

Ingredients:

- 2 large zucchinis, sliced into 1/4 inch rounds
- 1 tablespoon olive oil
- 1 teaspoon dried basil
- 1 teaspoon dried oregano
- 1/2 teaspoon garlic powder
- 1/4 teaspoon ground black pepper
- 1 tablespoon fresh parsley, finely chopped
- Fresh lemon wedges for serving

Directions:

1. In a bowl, toss the zucchini rounds with olive oil, basil, oregano, garlic powder, and black pepper until evenly coated.
2. Preheat the air fryer to 380°F (193°C). Place the zucchini rounds ina single layer in the air fryer basket. Air fry for 3 minutes, then flip the zucchini rounds and continue to air fry for another 4 minutes until they are tender and have grill marks.
3. Once cooked, sprinkle the zucchini with fresh parsley and red pepper flakes if desired.
4. Serve the vegetables with fresh lemon wedges on the side.

Nutrition information (per serving):

Calories: 50 kcal | Sodium: 10 mg | Cholesterol: 0 mg | Protein: 1.5 g | Fat: 3.5 g | Carbohydrates: 4 g

Notes:

Prep. Time: 10 min   Cook Time: 15 min   Service: 4

Berry Crème Brûlée

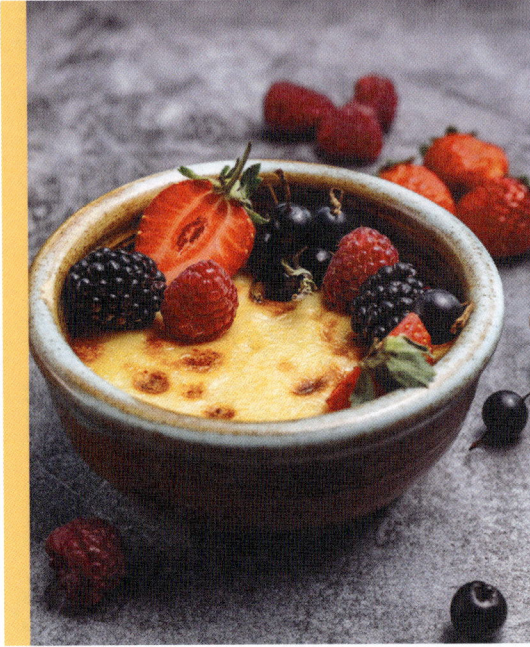

Ingredients:

- 1 cup heavy cream
- 1 teaspoon vanilla extract
- 1/4 cup granulated sugar, including extra for topping
- 4 large egg yolks
- 1/2 cup mixed berries (strawberries, raspberries, blackberries)
- Mint leaves for garnish

Directions:

1. Pour the heavy cream in a small, heat-safe dish. Add the vanilla extract to the cream.
2. Preheat the air fryer to 300°F (150°C). Place the dish in the air fryer basket and heat the cream for about 3-4 minutes or just until warm. Be careful not to let it come to a boil.
3. Combine the sugar and egg yolks, whisking them together until you achieve a light and thickened consistency. Gradually poor the warmed cream into the egg yolk mixture to temper the eggs and avoid cooking them.
4. Gently fold in the mixed berries, being careful not to break them.
5. Evenly distribute the custard mixture among four ramekins. Place the ramekins in the air fryer basket.
6. Air fry at 300°F (150°C) for 12-15 minutes, or until the custards are just set.
7. Once done, remove the ramekins from the air fryer with caution. Allow them to cool to room temperature. Then, refrigerate for at least 2 hours or until fully set.

Nutrition information (per serving):
Calories: 290 kcal | Sodium: 50 mg | Cholesterol: 220 mg | Protein: 4 g| Fat: 26 g | Carbohydrates: 10 g

Notes:

Prep. Time: 15 min   Cook Time: 25 min   Service: 4

Banana Bread

Ingredients:

- 3 ripe bananas, mashed
- 1/3 cup melted unsalted butter
- 1/2 cup maple syrup
- 1 teaspoon vanilla extract
- 1 egg, beaten
- 1 teaspoon baking soda
- 1 1/2 cups of whole wheat flour

Directions:

1. Mix in the mashed bananas with the melted butter, vanilla extract, maple syrup, and beaten egg until well combined. Then, add the baking soda evenly over the mixture and blend in.
2. Add the whole wheat flour, mixing until the flour disappears.
3. Pour the batter into a greased air fryer safe baking pan that fits in your air fryer basket.
4. Set the air fryer to 160°C (320°F) and bake for 20-25 minutes. It is ready when a toothpick is inserted into the center of the dish and comes out clean.
5. Allow the banana bread to cool for several minutes before slicing and serving.

Nutrition information (per serving):
Calories: 580 kcal | Sodium: 30 mg | Cholesterol: 88 mg | Protein:10 g | Fat: 18 g | Carbohydrates: 98 g

Notes:

Prep. Time: 11 min   Cook Time: 15 min   Service: 4

Chocolate Brownies

Ingredients:

- 1 cup all-purpose flour
- 1 cup granulated sugar
- 1/2 cup unsweetened cocoa powder
- 1/2 teaspoon baking powder
- 1/2 cup unsalted butter, melted
- 2 large eggs
- 1 teaspoon vanilla extract
- 1/2 cup dark chocolate chips

Directions:

1. In a large bowl, toss the flour, sugar, baking powder, and cocoa powder.
2. In another bowl, combine the eggs, melted butter, and vanilla extract until well combined.
3. Combine the wet ingredients with the dry ingredients, and stir until just mixed. Fold in the chocolate chips.
4. Set the air fryer to 160°C (320°F). Pour the brownie batter into a greased air fryer-safe pan that fits into your air fryer basket and cook for15-20 minutes, or until a toothpick inserted into the center comes out with a few moist crumbs.
5. Next, allow the brownies to cool in the pan before cutting into squares.

Nutrition information (per serving):

Calories: 480 kcal | Sodium: 60 mg | Cholesterol: 110 mg | Protein:6 g | Fat: 28 g | Carbohydrates: 58 g

Notes:

Prep. Time: 15 min	Cook Time: 10 min	Service: 4

Air Fryer Doughnuts

Ingredients:

- 1 cup all-purpose flour
- 1/4 cup granulated sugar
- 1 teaspoon low-sodium baking powder
- 1/4 teaspoon nutmeg
- 1/8 teaspoon cinnamon
- 1/2 cup milk
- 1 egg
- 1 tablespoon unsalted butter, melted
- 1 teaspoon vanilla extract
- Powdered sugar for dusting
- Non-stick cooking spray

Directions:

1. In a bowl, combine the yeast, flour, and sugar.
2. In another bowl, whisk together the warm milk, melted butter, egg, and vanilla extract until well combined. Next, slowly incorporate the wet ingredients into the dry ones until you form a smooth dough.
3. On a surface dusted with flour, roll out the dough to abut 1/2 inch thick. Use a doughnut cutter or a large and a smaller biscuit cutter to cut out the doughnuts and their holes.
4. Preheat the air fryer to 180°C (350°F). Spray the air fryer basket with non-stick cooking spray. Place the doughnuts in the air fryer basket in a single layer, making sure they are not touching.
5. Air fry the donuts for 5-7 minutes or until they turn golden brown and are fully baked, flipping them over halfway through the cooking time.
6. Dust the desert with powdered sugar while still warm.

Nutrition information (per serving):
Calories: 180 kcal | Sodium: 20 mg | Cholesterol: 47 mg | Protein:5 g | Fat: 4 g | Carbohydrates: 30 g

Notes:

Prep. Time: 15 min   Cook Time: 10 min   Service: 4

Pineapple Danish Pastries

Ingredients:

- 1 sheet puff pastry, thawed
- 1/2 cup pineapple preserves
- 1/4 cup cream cheese, softened
- 1 tablespoon honey
- 1 egg, beaten with 1 tablespoon water

Directions:

1. Roll out the puff pastry sheet. Cut it into 4 equal squares. In the center of each square, place a tablespoon of pineapple preserves and a tablespoon of cream cheese.
2. Fold the corners of the pastry squares towards the center, slightly overlapping the filling, to create a pinwheel shape. Brush the pastries with the egg wash for a golden finish.
3. Preheat the air fryer to 190°C (375°F). Place the pastries in the air fryer basket without overlapping, and cook for 8-10 minutes or until puffed and golden brown.
4. Once done, let them cool for a few minutes before serving.

Nutrition information (per serving):
Calories: 320 kcal | Sodium: 125 mg | Cholesterol: 31 mg | Protein:5 g | Fat: 20 g | Carbohydrates: 33 g

Notes:

Prep. Time: 17 min   Cook Time: 15 min   Service: 4

Almond Biscotti

Ingredients:

- 1 1/2 cups all-purpose flour
- 1/2 cup whole wheat flour
- 1 teaspoon baking powder
- 2/3 cup sugar
- 2 large eggs
- 1 teaspoon vanilla extract
- 1/2 teaspoon almond extract
- 1 cup whole almonds

Directions:

1. Whisk the baking powder, whole wheat flour, all-purpose flour.
2. In a separate bowl, beat the vanilla extract, sugar, eggs, and almond extract until well combined.
3. Slowly incorporate the wet ingredients into the dry ones until you form a smooth dough. Fold in the almonds. Form the dough into a log shape and place it on a lightly greased air fryer basket.
4. Preheat the air fryer to 160°C (320°F). Air fry the dough for 10-12minutes or until firm to the touch.
6. Remove it from the air fryer and let cool for a few minutes. Then, cut into 1/2-inch thick diagonal slices.
6. Place the slices back in the air fryer. Cook for an additional 3-4minutes on each side or until they are crisp and golden brown.

Nutrition information (per serving):
Calories: 280 kcal | Sodium: 60 mg | Cholesterol: 93 mg | Protein:8 g | Fat: 10 g | Carbohydrates: 42 g

Notes:

Prep. Time: 5 min | Cook Time: 8 min | Service: 4

Honey-Cinnamon Grilled Bananas

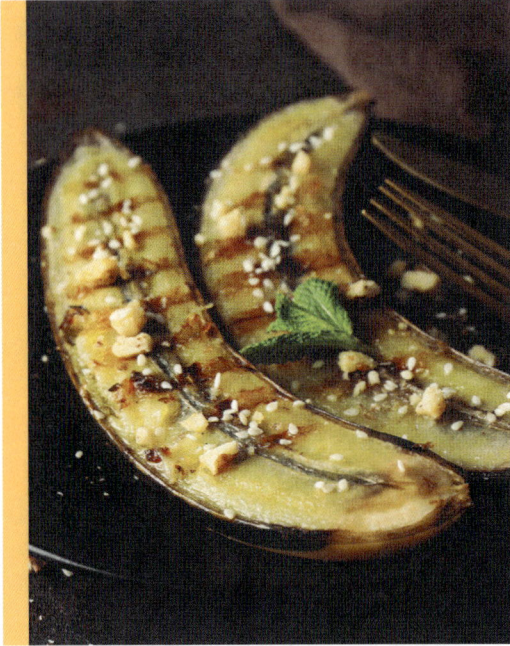

Ingredients:

- 2 large ripe bananas
- 2 teaspoons honey
- 1/2 teaspoon ground cinnamon
- 1 tablespoon chopped walnuts
- Fresh mint leaves for garnish

Directions:

1. Slice the bananas in half lengthwise, leaving the peel on.
2. Gently brush the cut side of the bananas with honey, then sprinkle evenly with ground cinnamon.
3. Preheat the air fryer to 375°F (190°C). Place the banana halves in the Air Fryer basket, cut side up, and cook for about 6-8 minutes.
4. garnish the grilled bananas with fresh mint leaves.

Nutrition information (per serving):

Calories: 105 kcal | Sodium: 1 mg | Cholesterol: 0 mg | Protein: 1 g | Fat:1.5 g | Carbohydrates: 27 g

Notes:

Prep. Time: 12 min	Cook Time: 20 min	Service: 4

Cinnamon Apple Cake Squares

Ingredients:

- 1 1/2 cups all-purpose flour
- 1/2 cup granulated sugar
- 1 1/2 teaspoons baking powder
- 1/2 teaspoon baking soda
- 1 teaspoon ground cinnamon
- 1/4 teaspoon ground nutmeg
- 2 large apples, cored and thinly sliced
- 2 large eggs
- 1/2 cup unsweetened applesauce
- 1/4 cup unsalted butter, melted
- 1 teaspoon vanilla extract

Directions:

1. In a large bowl, combine baking powder, baking soda, sugar, flour, cinnamon, and nutmeg.
2. In another bowl, blend eggs, applesauce, melted butter, and vanilla extract.
3. Merge the wet ingredients into the dry ingredients and stir until just combined. Gently fold in the apple slices.
4. Prep the air fryer basket with a sheet of parchment paper and pour the batter into the basket, spreading evenly.
5. Preheat the air fryer to 350°F (175°C). Bake for 20 minutes, or until toothpick inserted into the center comes out clean.
6. Allow it to cool slightly, then cut it into squares.

Nutrition information (per serving):
Calories: 350 kcal | Sodium: 150 mg | Cholesterol: 95 mg | Protein: 5 g| Fat: 12 g | Carbohydrates: 55 g

Notes:

Prep. Time: 13 min   Cook Time: 10 min   Service: 4

Low-Sodium Churros

Ingredients:

- 1 cup water
- 2 tablespoons sugar
- 2 tablespoons unsalted butter, melted
- 1 cup all-purpose flour
- 1 teaspoon vanilla extract
- 1 egg
- Cooking spray for greasing
- Cinnamon sugar for coating (1/4 cup sugar mixed with 1 teaspoon ground cinnamon)
- Chocolate sauce for dipping

Directions:

1. In a small saucepan, combine water, melted butter, and sugar. Bring to a boil over medium heat. Lower the heat to a simmer and quickly stir in the flour, mixing until it forms a cohesive ball.
2. Take the pan off the heat and let the dough cool down for a few minutes. Stir in the vanilla extract and egg, beating the mixture until it's smooth and fully combined. Place the dough into a piping bag that is equipped with a sizable star-shaped nozzle.
3. Pipe the dough into 6-inch long churros and place them in the air fryer basket. Make sure they do not touch. Lightly spray with cooking spray.
4. Preheat the air fryer to 190°C (375°F). Air fry for about 10 minutes or until golden brown, turning halfway through cooking. Remove from the air fryer and roll in cinnamon sugar to coat.
5. Serve with chocolate sauce for dipping.

Nutrition information (per serving):
Calories: 200 kcal | Sodium: 15 mg | Cholesterol: 40 mg | Protein:4 g | Fat: 6 g | Carbohydrates: 34 g

Notes:

Prep. Time: 12 min   Cook Time: 10 min   Service: 4

Rustic Pear Tart

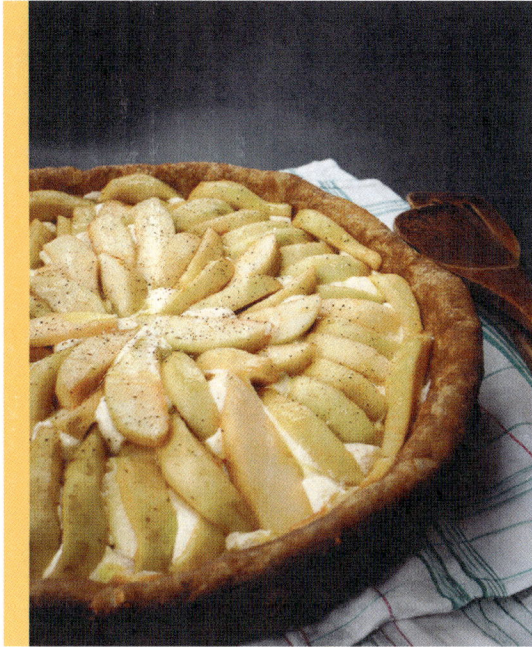

Ingredients:

- 1 sheet of low-sodium puff pastry, thawed
- 3 ripe pears, cored and thinly sliced
- 1 tablespoon lemon juice
- 2 tablespoons maple syrup
- 1/2 teaspoon ground cinnamon
- 1/4 teaspoon ground nutmeg
- 1 teaspoon vanilla extract
- Non-stick cooking spray

Directions:

1. Carefully lay out the puff pastry on a surface dusted with a bit of flour. Roll it out if necessary to ensure it fits your air fryer basket.
2. In a bowl, toss the pear slices with lemon juice, honey, cinnamon, nutmeg, and vanilla extract until well-coated.
3. Place one pear slice at a time in a circular pattern on the puff pastry, and gently fold the pastry's edges over the pears to create a rustic edge. Arrange the remaining pear slices onto the puff pastry, making sure to leave a small margin around the edges.
4. Preheat the air fryer to 350°F (175°C). Spray the basket with cooking spray. Transfer the prepared tart to the air fryer basket. Cook for approximately 20 minutes or until the pastry is golden and puffed.
5. Let the tart to cool before serving.

Nutrition information (per serving):
Calories: 320 kcal | Sodium: 70 mg | Cholesterol: 0 mg | Protein:3 g | Fat: 15 g | Carbohydrates: 45 g

Notes:

Prep. Time: 14 min   Cook Time: 15 min   Service: 4

Cinnamon Rolls

Ingredients:

- 1 cup all-purpose flour
- 2 tablespoons sugar
- 1 1/2 teaspoons low-sodium baking powder
- 1/4 cup unsalted butter, cubed, cold
- 1/3 cup milk

Filling:
- 1 tablespoon unsalted butter, melted
- 2 tablespoons brown sugar
- 1 tablespoon ground cinnamon

Icing:
- 1/2 cup powdered sugar
- 1 tablespoon milk
- 1/4 teaspoon vanilla extract

Directions:

1. In a bowl, combine the baking powder, flour, and sugar. Next, cut in the cold butter until the mixture resembles coarse crumbs. Gradually add milk to form a dough.
2. Next, on a floured surface, roll the dough into 1/4 inch thick rectangle. Then, spread the melted butter over the dough. Sprinkle evenly with cinnamon and brown sugar. Roll the dough tightly from the long end and slice it into 4 equal rolls.
3. Preheat the air fryer to 350°F (175°C). Place the rolls in the air fryer basket, leaving space between them for expansion. Cook for 12-15 minutes or until golden brown and cooked through.
4. While the rolls are cooking, whisk together the icing ingredients until smooth. Drizzle the warm cinnamon rolls with the icing before serving.

Nutrition information (per serving):
Calories: 300 kcal | Sodium: 75 mg | Cholesterol: 30 mg | Protein: 4 g | Fat: 12 g | Carbohydrates: 46 g

Notes:

Prep. Time: 12 min   Cook Time: 15 min   Service: 4

Raspberry Crumble Bars

Ingredients:

- 1 cup all-purpose flour
- 1/4 cup granulated sugar
- 1/4 cup brown sugar, packed
- 1/2 cup unsalted butter, cold, cubed
- 1/2 teaspoon baking powder
- 1 cup fresh raspberries
- 2 tablespoons cornstarch
- 2 tablespoons unsweetened raspberry jam
- Non-stick cooking spray

Directions:

1. In a mixing bowl, combine granulated sugar, brown sugar, flour, and baking powder. Add cold cubed butter and mix until the mixture resembles coarse crumbs.
2. Take 3/4 of the crumble mixture and press it into a parchment-lined air fryer basket to form a base.
3. In a separate bowl, gently toss raspberries with cornstarch and unsweetened raspberry jam. Spread this mixture over the crumble base. Sprinkle the remaining crumble mixture on top of the raspberry layer.
4. Preheat the air fryer to 360°F (182°C). Place the basket in the air fryer and cook for about 15 minutes or until the top is golden brown.
5. Let it cool before cutting it into portions.

Nutrition information (per serving):
Calories: 400 kcal | Sodium: 5 mg | Cholesterol: 61 mg | Protein:4 g | Fat: 22 g | Carbohydrates:50 g

Notes:

Conclusion

As our culinary journey draws to a close, we hope you've been inspired and that your table has been graced with new flavors, all while supporting your health and well-being. Our journey through low-sodium cooking using an air fryer was more than just about recipes; it was about discovering that healthful eating can indeed be delicious and effortless.

Remember, each meal you've prepared from this book is a step towards a healthier, more lively version of yourself. We encourage you to keep exploring, keep tasting, and keep enjoying the art of cooking. May these recipes become staples in your kitchen, bringing joy and health to you and your loved ones.

Thank you for allowing us to be a part of your kitchen. And Happy Cooking!

And, one more…

Please let us know if this cookbook was helpful to you in any way by leaving a review on Amazon.
It will take only a few minutes to share your thoughts:

1. Log into your Amazon account.
2. Go to "Accounts & Lists" > "Your Orders."
3. Find our cookbook and select "Write a Product Review.

Made in the USA
Monee, IL
06 May 2024

844d27df-4e0f-43ba-81a9-af906df6b74cR01